942.75

MINING MEMORIES

AN ILLUSTRATED RECORD OF COAL MINING IN ST. HELENS

GEOFF SIMM
IAN WINSTANLEY

ST. HELENS METROPOLITAN
BOROUGH COUNCIL
COMMUNITY LEISURE
DEPARTMENT
ST. HELENS, ENGLAND 1990

First Published by
St. Helens Metropolitan Borough Council
Community Leisure Department 1990

Century House, Hardshaw Street, St. Helens
Merseyside, England WA10 1RN

This book is computer typeset on an
Apple Macintosh IIcx System
in 9/12pt New Baskerville.

Designed, computer typeset & printed
in Great Britain
by Colourplan Design & Print,
St. Helens, Merseyside, England.

ISBN: 0 9511881 1 9

COLIN WELLAND

I'd come from Liverpool at the age of six and found myself at school in a village of strange accents and steel-tipped clogs. We waited by a pie shop for the red Lancashire United bus home. From its window, stared the saucer eyes of a Brylcreemed boxer hunched over his gloves. Peter Kane ate Pilling's Pies. Crouched on the pavement were black-faced men with red lips and pink eyes, helmets perched jauntily and snap tins worn low with the arrogance of gunslingers. They talked in a deep, low burr, their language to me a mystery, yet completely without threat, they breathed strength, reliability, even gentleness.

When the bus came, we were denied the upstairs. That was *their* domain and we'd sit in the bench-seats by the door gazing up at the mirror on the stairs into a forbidden world of smoke, scraping irons and throaty laughter.

They were miners and as I grew older amongst them I learned to respect, admire, even love them for the brave, abused yet 'salt-of-the-earth' men that they were. In those days, the green, flat wheatfields were dotted with winding gear. The only signs of the tunnelling thousands of feet below. It was monstrous labour to ask of men and yet its very nature created communities which were inter-reliant and painfully close — so close that closed doors just did not exist, all laughter was the whole street's and shoulders to cry on were a multitude.

A friend of mine, a well-known actor, went back to the site of his old granny's house near Wigan. It had been demolished. Only a few terraced houses remained. As he stood there remembering, the tears rolled down his cheeks. A door opened and an elderly neighbour poked out her head.

"Eee Kenneth lad," she said "Thee a television star skrykin' in middle o' street. Cum in an' 'ave a cup o' tea."

Miners, their grannies, their wives, their kids, they and their like made our little acre special. This friendliness, stoicism, courage and generosity is the envy of the nation. I have only been down a pit once, but terrified, crouched in a tunnel three feet high with a thousand feet of muck wheezing above me. It dawned that if you're *not* friendly, stoic, courageous and above all, generous you've no right being down there... Without them you'd certainly never survive!

So thank you for mining and its men. We're proud of you and I, for one, am delighted that your proud history is now being celebrated in this unique way.

COLIN WELLAND

MARIE E. RIMMER

St. Helens is the town of my birth and upbringing, and I like many others, have seen much change in recent years. To many, the most significant change was perhaps the formation of a new borough in 1974, creating a new St. Helens.

However, throughout the changes, one of the strongest historical and social links which bind the people of St. Helens together must be our mining heritage. It is well known that the mining industry generated among it's workers the closest of bonds. The fellowship which was necessary in olden times for survival underground was reflected in the strongest sense of identity among the mining communities which grew up around the pits.

It is startling to reflect that the history of mining in the area stretches back so far that this book can be published to celebrate 450 years of deep coal mining in St. Helens. Since the 1540's at least, coal mining has been at the centre of economic life and history of the town. Now, in this book, we have the latest record of that history.

The photograph of the 'Pit Brow Lasses' from Ashtons Green shows that there is clearly no sense of wealth. Shawls are their only protection from the coal dust and the heavy clothes keep out the cold and harsh environment in which they lived and worked. Yet, their poise and smile show us, in a real sense, that they possess an inner strength, a power and drive which was necessary to sustain such hard conditions and tragedies that 'pit-life' brought. We can only ponder on what their thoughts might have been.

Today, coal continues to be one of the earth's most valuable resources. Nowadays, only 2 pits remain in St. Helens, at Parkside and Sutton Manor. Happily they are rich and efficient and will continue to provide employment for our people and energy for our country.

Throughout this book the research undertaken by Geoff and Ian will help reflect through the words and pictures, on the magnificent history of our mining industry, and the people who have laboured over the centuries to make the earth give up this gift to us.

Marie. E. Rimmer

COUNCILLOR MARIE E. RIMMER
Leader of St. Helens Metropolitan Borough Council

THE AUTHORS

GEOFF SIMM

Geoff is a colliery electrician at Parkside Colliery, Newton-le-Willows. He was educated at Newton Secondary Modern School and Newton Technical College and for many years at the St.Helens College of Further Education.

He is secretary of The Newton Historical Society and has been involved in local history for over ten years.

IAN WINSTANLEY

Ian is a retired teacher who was born in Haydock and went to Richard Evans County Primary School and Ashton-in-Makerfield Grammar School. He started his career at Selwyn Jones County Secondary School, Newton-le-Willows and worked there for seven years before moving to Horwich.

He now lives in Ashton-in-Makerfield and spends much of his time researching the collieries of Ashton, Haydock and St. Helens.

AUTHOR'S NOTE

We were asked by St.Helens Community Leisure Department to produce a book on Mining in St. Helens for the Mining 1990 Project, celebrating the history of mining and mining people in St. Helens that will be held in the Borough in September 1990.

We have approached the task using local sources wherever possible and we are indebted to the people of the town who have made their personal archives available to us. The local newspapers at the Local History and Archives Library, are a mine of information, if you will pardon the pun.

There are many tragic accidents recorded in these pages and they form a large part of the text but there is much to be learned about the pattern of mining developments in these glimpses of our mining history.

At the back of the book there is an index to references of mining developments and a glossary of mining terms.

As we know from our frequent visits to libraries, many people are interested in the history of their family name and we have included an index of surnames.

We hope that the book lives up to it's title 'A Record of Mining in St. Helens' and will both stir memories for the elderly and inform the young.

Geoff Simm
Ian Winstanley
January 1990.

ACKNOWLEDGEMENTS

The authors are indebted to the following institutions for their help and cooperation in compiling this book:-

St.Helens Local History and
Archives Library. (St.HLH&AL)
The Warrington Guardian.
Wigan Reference Library.
Salford Mining Museum. (SMM)
Newton-le-Willows Library.
The 'St. Helens Reporter'.
The 'Star'.
British Coal. (BC)
Wigan Technical College Library.
Pilkingtons plc.
The Burtonwood Brewery.

There are many individuals, without whose help, the book would not have been completed. We include a list of those people who have donated material that is included in the book and we would like to record our appreciation to all who have helped in any way in it's compilation and production.

F.Armstrong.
K.Ashton.
J.Atherton.
F.Bennett.
Mrs. Bentham.
W.Bond.
Mr. Boon
A.Davis.
Mr. Dobson.
Mr. Griffiths.
W.Hilton.
J.Holden.
Mr. Hughes.
J.Jennison.
R.Jones.
G.Kilshaw.
Mr. and Mrs.Lesham.
Mr. and Mrs.Lever.
L.McDonald.
N.McGuirk.
Mr. Maddison.
Mrs.Morris.
Mr. and Mrs. Pilling.
T.Redmond.
E.Shaw.
Mr. and Mrs.Sumner.
A.Whalley.
M.Wilson.

To the memory of the men,
women and children who have worked in
the town's mines

Extract from the letter sent by Mr. Samuel
Driffield, the Lancashire County Coroner,
to the inquest into the Lyme Pit Explosion,
February 1930.

*"The Lancashire collier is a brave fellow, a
man of character, and one who is always
prepared to carry out his duty to the best of his
ability. He will always do anyone a good turn. I
have the greatest admiration for the Lancashire
collier."*

C O N T E N T S

ST HELENS — Traditionally known for its association with the glass industry, was founded by a different product entirely — COAL.

It was with coal that the industrial history of the town really began. Previous to the exploitation of coal, St.Helens was merely a chapel at the side of a crossroads. As we look back to the sixteenth century, we find Richard Bold, a local landowner, mining on Sutton Heath. The Bolds had the right to mine coal for their own use, but began to produce on a commercial basis. For that reason Richard Bold was sued by the Sutton landowners, led by the Eltonhead Family. During the court proceedings of the 1580's, a series of depositions were taken from local people. The most interesting of those depositions being:-

Robert Norman deposes:– *"coal pits have been dug on the said common and wastes called Sutton Heath distant from the house of the said Richard Eltonhead seventy roods, and that the said coal pits were sunk by Richard Eltonhead, the defendant's father, forty years ago by the licence of Richard Bolde, the complainant's father".*

Thomas Sherlocke, of Rainhill, husbandman, aged seventy, deposes:- *"about fifty years ago a coal pit was digged upon a certain common within the said manor of Sutton called Sutton Heath, near the house of the said Richard Eltonhead, by Lady Bolde for and on behalf of her son, the complainants father. He remembers this because his father had a colt drowned in the same coal pit whereof he made complaint unto Lady Bolde who compensated him."*

Gilbert Parker, deposes:- *" that he knows that there were coal pits digged upon Sutton Heath near the said Eltonhead's house about thirty years ago. He knows this because he was servant at Bold and brought meat to the workmen at the said coal pit and fetched coals to Bolde."*

Lawrence Muche, of Sutton, husbandman, aged eighty-three, deposes:- *"that he knows a certain place in Sutton called and known by the name of Pawghden or Pawghden Brooke, and says that the same goes westward from the coal pits and runs eastward upon the south side of the demesne lands of the said Richard Eltonhead in Sutton and so to Myles Peerson's, and from there to the new mill in Sutton aforesaid. He has known the same for forty years."*

The proceedings stretched over thirty years, with the two families finally coming to an agreement in the 1630's.

The previous depositions are documentary evidence that coal mining did begin in the St Helens area about 450 years ago. This is the earliest surviving evidence and it is possible that coal mining began even earlier than that date.

In the scant evidence from the seventeenth century we find reports of coal mining springing up in small pockets around the St. Helens area, Sutton, Windle, Parr and Eccleston.

It was realised by the end of the century that large amounts of coal were required by the Cheshire saltfields, which the coal proprietors of the St. Helens area provided in ever increasing amounts. It was this combination of coal and salt that brought money in to develop the town in the eighteenth and nineteenth centuries.

By the eighteenth century coal was also required in Liverpool, for the newly opened Salt Works. This connection with Liverpool, which became closer after the construction of the Sankey Canal, was one of the major factors in the development of the town.

In the eighteenth century there was great competition in the coalfield and the area abounded with such characters as Sarah Clayton in Parr, the Legh family in Haydock, the Case family in Whiston and Sutton, the Cotham and Baldwin families in Windle, James Orrell in Blackbrook and of course John Mackay in Ravenhead. Names that still live with us today, but their connection with the town has faded into history.

At the beginning of that century the coal trade relied on the precarious road transport to the various markets, but the arrival of the Sankey Canal in the 1750's altered all that. The Sankey Canal, which was instigated by the Liverpool merchants, enabled the coal from the St. Helens area to reach the markets in Liverpool and Northwich, quickly and throughout the year. The original intention was to make the Sankey Brook navigable, but during it's construction a cut, or canal, was produced along its complete length. It was estimated in the 1770's that 90,000 tons of coal passed along the canal during one year. The eighteenth century coalfield, with the canal, and the connection with Liverpool, produced the town we know today.

It was only in the nineteenth century that detailed documentation and recording of collieries really began. The Inspectors of Mines were introduced in the 1840's and first produced detailed reports from 1850. The arrival of photography at about the same time has enabled the authors to compile this book, which is a record of coal mining in St.Helens.

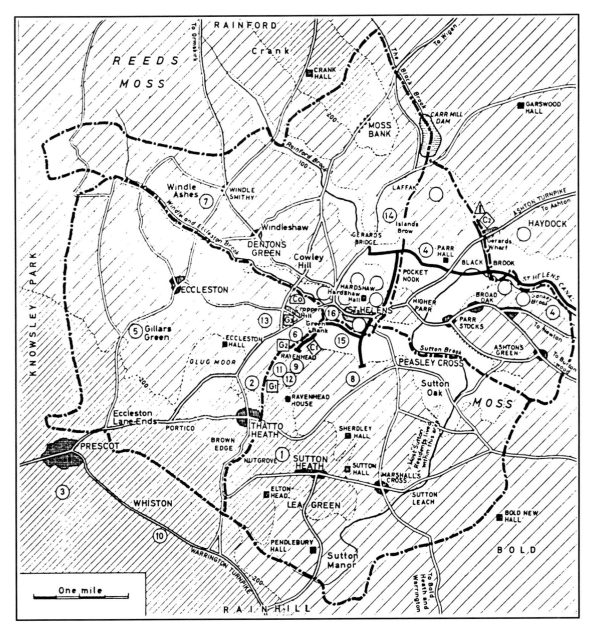

THE MAIN COLLIERIES (Approximate Sites)

① The first area mined for coal, 1540
② Thatto Heath developments, Late 17th cent.
③ Prescot Hall mine
④ Sarah Clayton's Parr Collieries
⑤ Gillars Green mines, 1750
⑥ Dagnall's Eccleston mines, 1746-56
⑦ Windle Ashes mines, 1760-66
⑧ Mackay's Burtonhead mines, 1762
⑨ Mackay's Ravenhead mines, 1768
⑩ The Carr Colliery (Case), 1769
⑪ Case Colliery, Ravenhead, 1769
⑫ Mackay's Collieries, 1765 and 1772
⑬ Case's Rushy Park mine, 1775
⑭ The Rushy Park Colliery, 1801
⑮ Ashton's Colliery, 1800 (later St. Helens Colliery)
⑯ Peter Berry's mine, 1758
◯ Other colliery sites, generally founded before 1780

◫ Land over 200 feet in height
◫ Land 100 - 200 feet in height
◻ Land under 100 feet in height

OTHER INDUSTRIES

GLASS WORKS

G₁ Thatto Heath Bottle Works
G₂ Ravenhead Plate Glass Works, 1773
G₃ The Mackay West & Co, Eccleston Street, 1792

COPPER WORKS

C₁ Pary's Mine Co. Ravenhead, 1780
C₂ Stanley Works, Blackbrook, 1772

IRON

⚠ Iron Slitting Mill

COTTON

Co The Eccleston Cotton Mill, 1784

Area most nearly built-up. (Most of the
district was covered by scattered dwellings)
Boundaries of the four townships
Canal
Streams

ROADS

Turnpikes
Other through roads
Local roads

ILLUSTRATIONS & PHOTOGRAPHS

ALEXANDRA COLLIERY

Situated on the corner of Alexandra Street and St. John Street. This colliery was sunk in 1867 by Pilkington Bros. The 'ST. HELENS STANDARD' records that on 4th. November 1867:- 'A new pit was sunk and in honour of the Princes of Wales was called the Alexandra Pit'. The Princess of Wales

These took the form of a small booklet that had to be issued to every man working in the colliery where he was employed and laid down in great detail what we today would call the conditions of work.

Many a collier found himself in court for breaking the 'Rules' and in the early part of the nineteenth century some were dealt with severely.

knocks and raised the cage to the place where the men got on. He then heard three knocks and raised the cage to the surface. When the cage stopped at the surface he saw the man on the top of the cage.

William Swift, the banksman, also gave evidence. The case was found proved and the accused was fined 20/- plus costs.

THE COLLIERY (Pilkingtons plc.)

visited the colliery during the sinking. The colliery was mentioned in the Inspector's Reports for 1873, 1888 and 1894.

Medical knowledge was not good in Victorian times.

From 'THE REPORT OF THE MINES INSPECTORS.'

1st May 1866.

Joseph Webster aged 51 years was getting some timber, when a stone fall inflicted a wound above the knee which was not considered dangerous at the time. Some weeks later the wound suppurated and he died in hospital 17th July.

By 1869, the working of coal mines had become such a complex operation that Her Majesty's Inspector of Mines had suggested that 'General' and 'Special Rules' be drawn up for each colliery.

From **'THE ST.HELENS STANDARD'**.
20th.March 1869.
BREAKING OF COLLIERY RULES.

At St.Helens Court, James Welding was charged with descending the shaft on top of the cage which was against the Colliery Rules at the Crop Pit at the Alexandra Colliery. Mr. Marsh prosecuted the accused. William Hobden, the underground manager of the pit, read the Rules of the Colliery and said that the accused had broken the first rule.

George Rothwell, the fireman, said that on Saturday evening it was his duty to see that all the men came out of the pit by seven and no one was allowed to ascend before that time.

Water was being wound at the time and Mathias Goulding, engineer in charge of the winding engine, said he knew the defendant. The cage was lowered a little lower than usual into the dib hole. He then heard four

From **'THE ST.HELENS STANDARD'**.
7th September 1869.
DANGEROUS ACT BY RECKLESS COLLIER

James Pate, collier, was charged at St Helens Court with pulling down a gob in the pit. A gob was reported to have been a piece of wood supporting the roof and he knocked it down as an act of bravado which caused a large fall.

Mr. Marsh prosecuting said that the act was punishable by transportation but he could be charged within the bye-laws of the colliery.

William Hobden, the underlooker, said the it was pulled down because he said that it interfered with the ventilation. Nineteen people were out of work until the place was repaired.

Pate was found guilty and sentenced to two months in prison with hard labour at Kirkdale Jail in Liverpool.

No colliery at this time was free from death and disaster and Alexandra colliery was no exception.

From the *'REPORT OF THE MINES INSPECTORS 1879'.*

The deaths of Peter Aspinall aged 32 years, Henry Norton aged 30 years, William Parr aged 50 years, Thomas Kay aged 45 years, James Webster aged 38 years, all of them colliers and Joseph Holland age 28 years and David Dixon aged 16 years both drawers, are recorded.

They were killed in an overwinding accident when the engine was started the wrong way round and the cage was taken up to the pulley. The rope broke and the cage fell to the bottom of the shaft. Joseph Naylor was the engineman who had been at the work for twenty years.

By 1915, strict examinations had to be passed before a man could take on the great responsibility of a fireman or deputy and a certificate like this represents many hours study at night school at St.Helens Mining School in the Gamble Institute or men even travelled to Wigan Mining and Technical College.

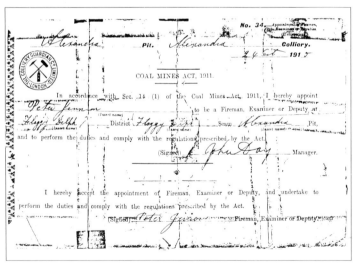

DEPUTIES CERTIFICATE (Mr. Jennion)

ASHES COLLIERY

This colliery was situated on the corner of the East Lancashire Road and the Rainford Bypass (Moss Lane). It first appeared in the records in 1759, when it was sunk by Charles Dagnall. The colliery only had a short life of about twelve years.

ASHTONS GREEN COLLIERY.

THE HEADGEARS OF ASHTONS GREEN COLLIERY (St.HLH&AL)

Situated between Fleet Lane and Derbyshire Hill Road. This colliery was in evidence in the 1780's, when it was purchased for £5,500 by a Mr. Blackburn of Liverpool. In the beginning of the nineteenth century James Orrell and Thomas Claughton worked the colliery very successfully. From then on it was run by John Shaw Leigh and his family, when it was raising 20,000 tons of coal annually. The colliery was taken over by Bromilow Foster & Co. in the 1880's and worked by them until its closure in 1931, when it employed 1,126 men.

From *'THE ST.HELENS NEWSPAPER'.*
9th. November 1861.
FATAL ACCIDENT AT ASHTONS GREEN.

On Tuesday last, coal waggons were being lowered by a boy seven years old. As he went to sprag the wheel it ran away and severely crushed him. It was stated at the inquest that a seven year old should not do such dangerous work.

From *'THE ST.HELENS LANTERN'.*
12th. June 1864
WHAT IS A COLLIER?

William Kay a collier, claimed damages from Bromilow & Company because he was taken off a job of coal getting and sent to a labourers job at the colliery. He said that he would not do the job and was dismissed but was cleared by the court. There were many miners present and the union bore the costs of the case.

From *'THE REPORT OF THE MINES INSPECTORS'.*
16th. March 1876.

Richard Grimes aged 40 years, a labourer, struck on the head by a winch handle and killed.

From *'THE REPORT OF THE MINES INSPECTORS'.*
5th. March 1877.

Richard Shepperd aged 64 years. A dataller. Strained himself while lifting a tub. Died 12th April.

From *'THE REPORT OF THE MINES INSPECTORS'.*
2nd. October 1901.

John Williams aged 48 years. A collier. In contravention of the bye-laws, the shotlighter allowed a collier to attach the cable to the fuse and the shotlighter appears to have fired the shot without taking steps to see that the collier was out of the way. He was still at the fuse when the shot was fired. He died on the 4th October.

From *'THE REPORT OF THE MINES INSPECTORS'.*

21st. June 1907.

DANGEROUS OCCURRENCES.

In the No.5 pit the capping of the ascending winding rope drew out of the cage and it fell down the shaft. It was stated that the catch holding the tubs in the cage had been put down causing one of the full tubs to fall out and another tub caught the wood work near the top of the shaft causing a sudden shock that caused the capping rope to give way.

Every colliery had it's own forge and blacksmith's shop which not only did running repairs to the machinery but, in may cases, manufactured machinery that was used in the colliery.

THE SAWMILLS AT ASHTONS GREEN COLLIERY ABOUT 1919 (St.HLH&AL)

BLACKSMITH AT WORK AT ASHTONS GREEN COLLIERY ABOUT 1919. IT IS THOUGHT THAT HE IS MR. PEARCE. (St.HLH&AL)

In the early part of the twentieth century, timber was extensively used underground to support the roof in the roads and workings and every colliery had it's own timber yard.

When the coal came to the surface it had to be sorted into size and this was done at the screens which were large mechanical riddles. From the screens it was usually loaded into railway waggons but this unusual photograph shows it being loaded into carts.

THE SCREENS AT ASHTONS GREEN COLLIERY ABOUT 1919 (St.HLH&AL)

BARTONS BANK COLLIERY

The colliery was situated between Watery Lane and the railway line. It was worked by Charles Dagnall in the 1750's, but had closed by 1839.

BLACKBROOK COLLIERY

The colliery was situated at the corner of Blackbrook Road, Chain Lane and Link Ave. It was being worked in the 1790's by James Orrell, the owner of the estate, who had been involved in coal mining for a number of years. The colliery had been working for a long time when the official records of the Inspectors of Mines first reported in 1850. It was owned by David Bromilow and, in 1843, it was reported that two men earned thirty four shillings a fortnight. The colliery was mentioned in 1860, when 30,000 tons of coal were being raised per year. At that time it was owned by Bromilow & Sothern. The colliery closed about 1863.

Methane gas which miners know as firedamp is always present in coal and was feared and respected. It is an inflammable gas on it's own but when mixed with a proportion of air, it becomes an explosive mixture which, if ignited, can become a killer.

From *'THE REPORT OF THE MINES INSPECTOR'*.
11th. October 1856.
EXPLOSION OF FIREDAMP AT BLACKBROOK COLLIERY.

Some firedamp that had accumulated in the goaf was accidentally fired by an inexperienced collier working with his lamp uncovered. The explosion did not extend much beyond the goaf but the coal was very dry and the explosion set it on fire. The flames spread rapidly to the extremity of the workings where a number of men and boys were employed.

The person who fired the gas escaped personal injury but the three others were suffocated by smoke and gases from the burning coal. One of the sufferers a boy of eighteen years has not been found.

Steam at high pressure has continually been forced into the workings which have been stopped since the accident but up to this time the fire had not been extinguished altogether.

In all probability the men might have put the fire out after it had ignited but they left their places and did not inform the underlooker until they reached the pit bottom by which time the fire had raged and spread a considerable length.

From *'THE ST.HELENS INTELLIGENCER'*.
25th. October 1856.

The inquest into the deaths of the three who were killed was held at the Royal Arms, Parr. It was stated that they met their deaths by chokedamp.

Lawrenson, who was the cause of the explosion, was working with a naked candle because the ventilation was good and was acting under the orders of Thomas Johnson the underlooker who, since the explosion had been discharged.

All the witnesses agreed that the ventilation was good. Mr. Higson the Inspector read the Rules of the Colliery relating to naked lights and the jury brought in a verdict of 'Accidental Death'.

From *'THE REPORT OF THE MINES INSPECTOR'*.
27th. January 1857.

Thomas Whittle, a drawer, was killed when he fell down the pit.

From *'THE ST.HELENS INTELLIGENCER'*.
31st. January 1857.

The inquest on Thomas Whittle, aged 11 years, was held at the Ship Inn owned by Mrs. Banks. The jury brought in a verdict of 'Accidental Death'.

From *'THE COLLIERY GUARDIAN'*.
27th. March 1858.
BREACH OF THE RULES.

At St.Helens Petty Sessions on Tuesday last, before the Chairman, Robert Neilson Esq., a full bench of magistrates heard Peter Bromilow charged with a breach of Special Rule 18, taking the top off his lamp and smoking down the pit where lamps are extensively used. He pleaded guilty.

Mr Molyneaux, the manager, stated that on the morning of the 16th. he was in the Rushy Park Mine and he saw him take the top off his lamp and light his pipe. There were one hundred men in the pit at the time and such an action put their lives at risk as there was a good chance that gas was present. He testified as to the accused good

character. He was strongly admonished and fined 20/- plus costs.

From *'THE ST.HELENS INTELLIGENCER'*.
14th. May 1859.

James Buckley, aged 66 years, a hooker-on at the Chain pit of the Blackbrook colliery had three fingers torn away and his arm fractured. He was in the act of hooking waggons on to the endless chain when the engine suddenly started and he was caught and dragged against some boxes. He lies in a precarious state

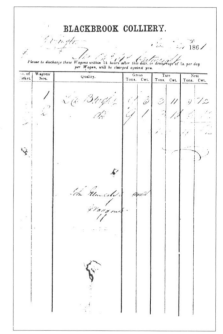

HEADING ON PAPER FROM 1861
(Mr. J. Atherton)

From *'THE ST.HELENS STANDARD'*.
21st. April 1866.
FUNERAL.

The funeral of the late Joseph Hill who was accidentally killed at Bromilow's colliery in Blackbrook took place last Saturday. The mortal remains were followed by numerous miners who showed their respect to the deceased by seeing him conveyed to his last resting place. All wore black sashes provided by the Miners Provident and Benefit Society. They conducted themselves with order and decorum.

It is hoped that the miners of Haydock and St.Helens will put themselves within the benefit of the Society

There were many instances of coal stealing from the collieries in the district and very often children were charged and appeared before the St Helens Bench. Not all were so lucky as Harriet Groves.

From *'THE ST.HELENS STANDARD'*.
8th. May 1869.

At the Magistrates Court in St. Helens, Harriet Groves stole 45lbs of coal from the Blackbrook colliery.

P.C.108 saw the accused with the coal she had taken from a coal waggon. She said that she thought it all right to take the coal as it was off the colliery premises.

The bench took a lenient view and dismissed the case.

BOLD COLLIERY

Situated on Bold Lane, this colliery was sunk in 1876 and production began in 1880. In 1873 the Inspector of Mines received a complaint concerning the state of the shaft which was in the course of being sunk. On visiting it the following day the owners promised to wall the shaft before sinking any further. This was done and carried on all to the bottom of the shaft. It was then owned by The Collins Green Colliery Co. It was closed in the 1930's and then reopened by the Sutton Heath & Lea Green Collieries Co. Ltd., when two of the shafts were deepened to 900 yards.

After Nationalisation, the N.C.B. completely reorganised the colliery, making it into one of the largest and most modern in the area. When the work was completed in 1956, the colliery was capable of producing over 700,000 tons of coal per year. Bold colliery closed soon after the 1984 Coal Strike, due to political and economic reasons.

From *'THE MINES INSPECTORS REPORT'*.
26th. January 1886.

Dominic Dalton aged 35 years, the banksman, was killed when he was going into the cage to get the loaded tubs out. By accident the engine crept and lifted the cage. He jumped out and a tub followed him and fell on him.

At the inquest reported in the Colliery Guardian 5th February 1886, it was stated that the cage suddenly went eight feet into the headgear. William Appleton, in charge of the brow, went into the engine house after the accident and thought that Marsden, the engineman, had on too much steam after oiling the valve. The verdict censured Marsden for not having showed enough care.

From *'THE MINES INSPECTORS REPORT'*.
10th. January 1878.
PROSECUTIONS.

At St.Helens Magistrates Court John Jones was charged with unramming a shot at the colliery. He was not in court as he had absconded.

From *'THE MINES INSPECTORS REPORT'*.
11th. February 1888.

William Storey aged 45 years, a blacksmith at the colliery was helping to put in a new cage and was standing near the pit mouth which was well lit when he was asked for some dome shackles. He stepped forward without thinking and fell down the pit.

In 1900 coal was won from the face with the collier's muscle wielding a pick and shovel. Underground photographs are very rare but this is believed to be at Bold colliery at about this date.

COLLIER GETTING COAL c1900 (BC)

The coal was hauled through the roads from the face by haulage engines that were powered by steam or compressed air. This photograph is believed to have been at Bold colliery about 1900.

GENERAL VIEW OF THE OLD COLLIERY (St.HLH&AL)

ENGINEMAN c1900 (BC)

PIT BROW GIRLS c1900 (BC)

In Loving Memory of

John M'Henry, age 14, John Swift, age 24,
Thos. Rothwell, age 14, Evan Davies, age 15
John Caveney, age 14,

Who lost their lives in the Cage Disaster at the Dold
Colliery, St. Helen's,

On Monday, January 16th, 1905.

Death to us short warning gave,   We cannot tell who next may fall,
Therefore be careful how you live,   Beneath Thy chast'ning rod ;
Prepare in time; do not delay,   One must be first, but let us all—
For we were quickly called away.   Prepare to meet our God.

REMEMBERANCE CARD OF THE VICTIMS (Mr. Kilshaw)

SCREENS c1900 (BC)

The 'screens' that graded the coal were often staffed by women. These were the famous 'Pit Brow Lasses'

From *'THE MINES INSPECTORS REPORT'*.
30th. July 1902.
Joseph Jones aged 33 years, a collier was killed when he was coming up the endless rope haulage. He was found dead against a bar. No one saw the accident but he was probably leaning on the tubs going up the brow and was caught by the bar.

On Monday, 16th January 1905, the colliery was the scene of a major disaster in the district when five people, most of them boys, were killed when the cage got out of control and crashed into a landing place. Thirteen others were injured and taken to St. Helens Hospital.

In the 1950's the colliery was extensively modernised and new headgears erected. Clockface Colliery can be seen in the background.

THE COLLIERY AFTER MODERNISATION IN THE 1950'S (Mr. Simm)

THE DEMOLITION OF THE HEADGEARS AT BOLD (St.HLH&AL)

A TYPICAL PAY SLIP FOR 1937 (Miss Williams)

In the 1930's day wage men did not earn a lot with which to bring up a family.

Some miners were trained to a high standard of First Aid and they were the only non-medical personnel that were allowed to administer morphine, provided they had the required certificate.

MORPHINE CERTIFICATE (Mr. Redmond)

BROADOAK COLLIERY

The colliery was situated close to Broad Oak Road. There was a colliery mentioned in this area in the 1790's, but the best reference to it appeared in 1832, when it transported the first coal along the St Helens and Runcorn Gap Railway. At that time it was owned by Bournes and Robinson. The colliery appears in the lists of mines in the Inspectors of Mines Reports for 1850 and 1855, but no later than 1873.

From **'THE ST.HELENS INTELLIGENCER'.**
6th. February 1850.
On Monday last at the colliery a boy named Hill had his head crushed while riding on a waggon in the shunt at breakfast time. He was on a tub where there was only a few inches between the roof and he looked out. Riding on the tubs was against the Rules of the Colliery.

From **'THE REPORT OF THE INSPECTOR OF MINES'.**
26th. July 1858.
Margaret Harrison, aged 14 years was employed on the pit bank and was run over by an empty coal truck above ground. The St. Helens Intelligencer reported that the inquest into her death was held at the Boars Head and a verdict of 'Accidental Death' was recorded.

The St. Helens Intelligencer reported that there was a strike at the colliery in August 1858. 'The colliers are on strike and there is no sight of agreement. The Colliers Society agreed to pay each man 10/- per week while they are out'.

On 13th. October 1858 the same paper reported;- 'The eight week strike has been terminated by the owners agreeing to give the men the same as the other colliers in the district. Thirty-six men went back to work and the others got their discharges so that they could get work in the district. This was a victory for the men. £100 has been paid out by the Colliers Society'.

Colliers actions at work could lead to severe action being taken against them.

From **'THE COLLIERY GUARDIAN'.**
20th. November 1858.
MANSLAUGHTER CHARGE.

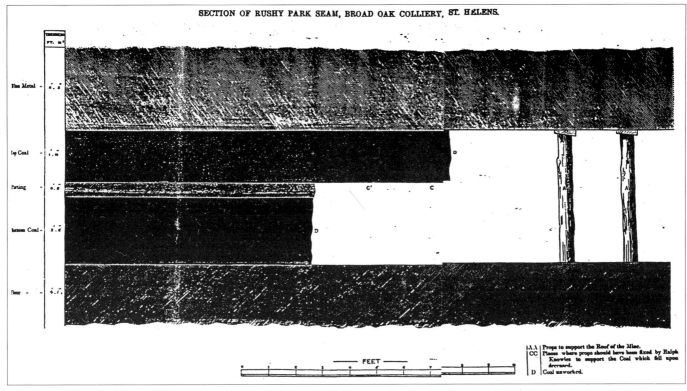

SECTION OF RUSHY PARK SEAM, BROAD OAK COLLIERY, ST. HELENS.

DIAGRAM FROM 'THE REPORT OF THE INSPECTOR OF MINES' (from Mr. Higsons report)

At the inquest held in Parr into the death of William Johnson aged 22 years who, last Friday was acting as drawer to Ralph Knowles in the Rushy Park Mine. Whilst engaged in working, a large fall of roof crushed him and killed him. Knowles was also injured about the body.

The jury brought in a verdict of manslaughter against Knowles. Bail was set at £40 for himself with two sureties of £20 each. Knowles was also a beer seller and lives in Sutton.

Knowles apparently left a large amount of the top coal unsupported and it was this that fell on his drawer.

BROOKFIELD COLLIERY

The colliery was mentioned in the 1873 Inspector's Report and was under the ownership of George Harris and Co. of St.Helens.

BURROWS LANE COLLIERY

The colliery was situated off Burrows Lane near Burrows Lane Farm. There is very little information about this colliery, but it was said to have been worked by Johnathan Case about 1753.

BURTONHEAD COLLIERY

The colliery was situated on the corner of Burtonhead Road and Sherdley Road. The colliery was mentioned in 1844 when it was auctioned by the owners, Clare and Co. It was also referred to by the 'Inspectors Report' of 1873 as being a drift mine.

CARR MILL COLLIERY or CARR MILL ARLEY

The colliery was situated on Lime Vale Road. It was owned by the Carr Mill Arley Colliery Co. Ltd. and thirty men worked there when it was closed in 1925.

CARRS COLLIERY

This was situated in Prescot and was reported as being sunk in 1873 by Carrs Colliery Co. In 1894 it employed 335 people and, according to the records, it closed in 1895.

CITY COLLIERY (WINDLE)

The colliery was situated off Bleak Hill Road. It was probably sunk to take advantage of the upsurge in coal prices of the early 1870's. It appeared in the 'Inspector's Report' for 1873 to be under the ownership of Mr. G. A. Bates of Windle. The colliery probably worked for only a short while and was closed by 1876.

CLOCKFACE COLLIERY

The colliery was situated on Gorsey Lane, Clockface. The No.1 and No.2 shafts were sunk initially in 1890 to a depth of 500 ft., but these were abandoned due to water problems. In 1904 the Wigan Coal and Iron Company took the colliery over. They turned No.1 shaft into a pumping pit and it dealt with over 700,000 gallons of water per day, with 500,000 gallons being sold to St. Helens Corporation. The Colliery was improved in the 1930's and the 1950's, but was forced to close down in 1966, when there were 638 men producing 169,000 tons of coal.

THE OLD PIT (The St. Helens Reporter)

From **'THE REPORT OF THE MINES INSPECTOR'.**
17th. July 1896.

Sinking operations were going on at the colliery when Andrew Neary aged 31 years, a sinker, was killed. They were tipping water out of the hoppet over the sinkers into the water trough, when the banksman slipped his hold on the hoppet and it upset water down the pit falling onto him and fatally injuring him.

From **'THE REPORT OF THE MINES INSPECTOR'.**
1923.

It was reported that a contractors man, who is not named, was injured by a fall of roof and eight days later while clearing the debris at the road end a large stone fell with no warning. The fireman had visited the place an hour before and ordered a prop and bar. The roof had been left too long with nothing to support it.

The colliery was modernised and the old wooden headgears replaced by steel ones.

THE HEADGEARS AND SCREENS (Mr. Simm)

THE LAMPROOM (BC)

There had been many improved versions of the miner's safety lamp since Davy, Stevenson and Clanny brought out their lamps in 1813. By the 1940's, collieries had 'lamp rooms' where the lamps were serviced and from which they were issued.

One great northern tradition was fully supported by the collieries in the area, the Colliery Brass Band. The photograph is of the 'Haydock Colliery Prize Band' which now plays as the Haydock Brass Band. The authors hope that someone will remember the photograph. Don't be shy. Give them a ring!

1926 was the year of the General Strike which was called for 5th. May. The troubles in the mining industry were recorded in the local papers.

From *'THE ST.HELENS REPORTER'*.
9th. April 1926.
MINERS AND THE CRISIS.
Bold and Clockface
500 Men under notice.
Many people picked coal from the colliery tips round the town to get some cheap fuel for themselves and to sell it. This was both dangerous and hazardous as they could find themselves in court.

From *'THE ST.HELENS REPORTER'*.
16th. April 1926.
DANGEROUS COAL TIP AT CLOCKFACE.
Serious damage to the colliery heap near Clockface was caused by people picking coal.

The dirt heap, which contains a good quantity of coal and on the tip are the railway lines on which run the waggons from the pithead to be tipped there.

It has been the custom for the people living round the colliery to visit the heap and purloin some coal.

The management had put up warning notices warning people of the consequences of raiding the heap but the practice

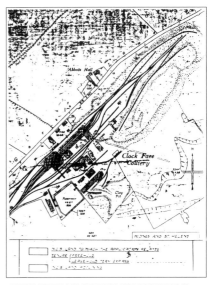

SURFACE PLAN OF THE COLLIERY 1962

continued to flourish wonderfully well, even when one of the raiders was buried and killed a few months ago it did not deter the rest.

On Monday about 150 people were engaged in raking and scratching along the tip for coal. The railway line at the top began to sink as the trains from the colliery weigh about 100 tons. Some pickers are not only stealing but doing such damage as will endanger the lives of other people.

The Company decided to take action and called the police and P.C. Johnson took the names of the people but he specially noted John Wareing, Frank Johnson and John Lacey who were damaging the heap.

At the St.Helens Police Court on Tuesday the Magistrate fined each offender 5/-.

A COLLIERY BAND (Mr. Simm)

COLLINS GREEN COLLIERY

There were shafts on the site from an early date. The colliery only appeared in the Inspector's Reports in the 1870's and was recorded as being owned by the Collins Green Colliery Co. By the 1880's this Company also worked Bold colliery.

In 1894 the number of people employed was 841 in the No.1 and the No.2 pits. There were also two other shafts, Nos. 3 and 4 which were used exclusively for pumping. The colliery closed in 1931 when it employed 256 people.

From *'THE REPORT OF THE MINES INSPECTOR'.*
8th. February 1897.

Michael Mullam aged 57 years, an ostler was going down the pit and the banksman, though on duty, was not present. Through some misunderstanding the cage was lowered before he was safe and he was crushed by the descending cage.

From *'THE REPORT OF THE MINES INSPECTOR'.*
2nd. August 1923.

At 9 am. in the second hour of the shift, James McGrail, a drawer aged 34 years was killed while filling coal tubs and a stone fell from the roof on him. The place was well

timbered and the stone fell from between two slips.

From *'THE NEWTON AND EARLESTOWN GUARDIAN'.*
13th. March 1931.
COLLINS GREEN COLLIERY.
Additional claim fails.

Judgement was given in a colliery compensation case held in St.Helens Court on Wednesday by Judge Morris. John Houghton was injured at the colliery on 22nd. March 1923 when top coal fell on him and hurt his head severely. He was off work for several months and received compensation but he returned to the colliery on 3rd. March 1925 when he was certified

THE OLD COLLINS GREEN COLLIERY (Burtonwood Brewery)

In 1878 the St.Helens Corporation wished to increase the water supply of drinking water to the town and pumping stations were made at the colliery. Drinking water for the town is still pumped from the disused shafts and the water is of excellent quality.

We are informed that the building in the foreground was one of the cottages along the Liverpool Manchester railway line that George Stevenson built. Sadly it has been demolished.

From *'THE REPORT OF THE MINES INSPECTOR'.*
23rd. November 1875.

It was reported that Matthew Hampson aged 45 years, a sinker and James McDonald aged 27 years, also a sinker were killed by bricks falling down the sinking shaft

CAGE AND SHAFT (SMM)

THE HEADGEARS (SMM)

The colliery was situated on City Road near the rugby ground. It was opened in 1821 and was referred to in 1829, as being near to the proposed Liverpool to Manchester Railway, a route that was later changed. The colliery was mentioned in the 'Inspectors Reports' for 1850 and 1855, when the owners were Caldwell and Thompson, who were also owners of Gerard's Bridge Colliery.

CRANK COLLIERY

This was in Rainford and mentioned in the Inspector's Reports in the 1860's and 70's as being owned by John Johnson and the Crank Colliery Co.

CROP AND DEEP COLLIERIES

In the old records, there are references to the 'Deep Colliery' to 'Crop Colliery' and to 'Crop and Deep Colliery'. The confusion arises from the fact that the shafts were often named as a pit and the names 'pit' and 'colliery' can mean the same thing. For example there are references to 'Chain Pit' but it is known that this was a shaft at the Blackbrook colliery. Crop Pit could be a shaft at the Alexandra Colliery and Deep pit could be another colliery. Crop pit could also refer to any shaft sunk into an outcrop, or 'crop', of a coal seam. (See St.Helens colliery.)

From *'THE REPORT OF THE MINES INSPECTOR'.*
22nd. March 1883.
Henry Brown aged 28 years, a fireman, was assisting to put some full tubs into the shunt at the bottom of an incline by which a journey was being drawn up by the engine when the tub at the end of the coupling

as suffering from mystagmus. From that time he had been employed on the surface and from March 1930 he was certified as not fit for work.

Proceedings had begun for the renewal of the compensation, and three medical men certified that he was no longer suffering from the result of his injuries. The judge said he had consulted a medical referee and he had to refuse the claim. The award was for the colliery company with costs

A cage was the means of transport down the shafts of collieries. Colliers will tell you, with a smile on their face, that it is like a modern lift, but no lift travels at the speed of a cage.

The colliery came to the end of it's useful life and was derelict for some time but it is still providing the town with drinking water.

COWLEY HILL COLLIERY

Gerards Bridge and Cowley Hill Collieries.
RUSHY PARK COAL.
St. Helens. 29th april 1843

LETTERHEAD FOR GERARD'S BRIDGE AND COWLEY HILL COLLIERIES (St.HLH&AL)

chain broke the trailer and the tubs ran back and killed him. The incline provided the necessary refuge places.

20th. April 1901.

George Woodward aged 27 years, a carpenter, was killed while putting a new rope on the main pulley in the engine house assisted by some others. The coupling rope caught the pulley shaft and before the men could shout the engine pulled the rope off the flywheel and it fell on him.

CROPPERS HILL COLLIERY

This was situated on Enfield Street. The colliery was first mentioned in the 'Hardshaw Colliery Letter Book' for 1805, and in 1845 it was owned by Bromilow, Brown and Jones. In the 1850's it was bought by James Radley, who made it a great success. The production of coal in the 1860's was given as 40,000 tons per year and was transported, by canal, to Liverpool or sold locally. For a time, (in it's history) ,it was known as 'Starvation Colliery', due to its unprofitability.

From *'THE WIGAN OBSERVER'.*
31st. September 1855.

Henry Ashall, a collier, was killed by falling fifteen yards down the shaft. They were in the habit of sliding down a plank which was steadied by chains. He was the last to come down and slipped off due to the chain being slack. The inquest recorded a verdict of 'accidental death'.

From *'THE REPORT OF THE MINES INSPECTOR'.*
23rd. January 1861.

George Pennington, a lad of 11 years of age, who was a waggoner at the pit, was killed by falling down the pit.

The following reference appeared in the 'COLLIERY GUARDIAN' dated 26th. January 1861.

'On Wednesday a youth, George Pennington, a drawer in the Flaggy Delf Mine was killed by falling 100 yards down the shaft. It appears that he had just ascended and lost his balance. His body was a horrible spectacle when it was recovered'.

From *'THE ST.HELENS STANDARD'.*
17th. February 1866.
COAL STEALING.

Bridget Glynn, Katherine Hallighan and Katherine Lynch were charged with stealing coal from the colliery owned by James Radley at Croppers Hill.

Mr. Swift appeared for the prosecution and Mr. Atkinson for the prisoner Lynch. It appeared from the evidence that for some time complaints had been received about large quantities of coal disappearing from the colliery while the flats were being loaded at the canal bank to such an extent that three tons of coal had been stolen out of a flat containing 70 tons.

P.C. Routledge had received instructions to watch the flats. Proceeding to the place about three o'clock he saw a cart of coal loaded from the flats and saw Bridget Glynn, a girl of about 10 years of age, attempt to knock a large piece of coal from the back of the cart with a stick. After several attempts she succeeded and she immediately picked up the coal and ran away with it, but was unfortunately apprehended by the police. On being taken into custody it was found that the coal weighed 17 lbs.

Between six and seven the same day, the police saw the two other prisoners going to the place and picking up several pieces of coal and putting them into their aprons. After being taken into custody one had 47 lbs of coal and the other 42 lbs

On the recommendation of Mr. Atkinson the Magistrates agreed that the cases should be heard separately and the Magistrates found them all guilty and sentenced Lynch and Hallighan to one month in prison. In the case of the prisoner Glynn it was believed that her mother had put her up to it and she was sent to prison for seven days.

ECCLESTON HALL COLLIERY

The colliery was situated on the Eccleston Hall Estate. Coal had been mined on the estate during the eighteenth century by the local squire and various lessees. A colliery is also mentioned in this area in the 1894 Inspector's Report, when it was owned by the Worsley Mesnes Colliery Co. The colliery employed about 300. The 'Colliery Guardian' referred to several shafts already sunk on the estate by former lessees of the minerals. Two of the shafts were used by the company to form part of their colliery. The colliery closed about 1910.

THE OPENING OF ECCLESTON HALL COLLIERY (St.HLH&AL)

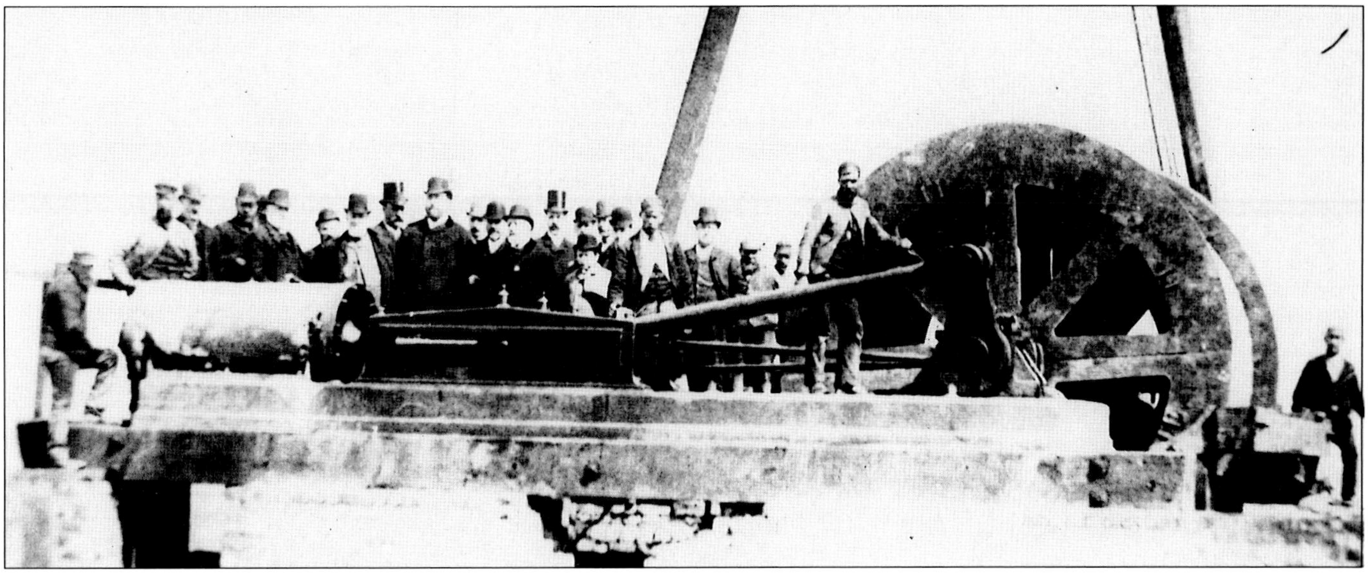

THE OPENING OF ECCLESTON HALL COLLIERY ENGINE (St.HLH&AL)

The opening of a new colliery was a great event in the district since it brought the prospect of new employment. The opening could be the re-opening of the old Gillars Green Colliery which closed in the 1880's

Here we get a good picture of the winding engine before the engine house was built around it.

A detailed description of the colliery and the engine appeared in the 'COLLIERY GUARDIAN' 30th. December 1892.

1204 **THE COLLIERY GUARDIAN.** **DECEMBER 30, 1892.**

Names of Coals.	Quantity in kilogrammes equivalent to 1,000 kilogs. of Cardiff coal.	Price of this quantity in francs.	Comparative value in francs deducted from column No. 2.	Quantities in kgr. consumed per hour and per square metre (10·76 square feet) of grate surface. Firing hard.	Ordinary firing.	Product of column 4 by column 5 proportional to the maximum speed.
1.	2.	3.	4.	5.	6.	7.
European Coals:—						
Cardiff	1,000	64 at Yokohama	1·00	115	90	115
Newcastle	1,200	Do.	0·83	132	112	109
Anzin	960	Do.	1·04	115	98	119
Rocher-Bleu	1,480	Do.	0·67	168	145	112
Anzin briquettes	988	Do.	1·01	122	98	123
Eastern Coals:—						
Saghalien	1,250	56	0·80	80	65	64
Poronaï	1,260	40	0·80	110 & upwards	70	88 & upwards
Takasima	1,220	36 at Nagasaki… 45 elsewhere	0·80 to 0·85	80	65	66
Hamaouza	1,230	52·50	0·80	85	70	68
Kara-su	1,330	52·50	0·75	90	75	67
Namazuka	1,340	52·50	0·75	90	75	67
Hayama	1,430	56·60	0·70	95	80	66
Yunochi	1,650	66	0·60	80	70	48
Chikijen	1,800	38·80	0·55	70	60	39
Houpe	2,200	38·80	0·45	70	60	39
Ke-lung	1,400	41	0·70	110 & upwards	70	77
Kabao	1,430	41	0·70	70	60	49
Tourane	1,430	41	0·70	70	60	49
Hong-Gac	1,430	41	0·70	70	60	49
Australian (average at quay)	1,290	55·40	0·80	110	90	88

THE LANCASHIRE COALFIELD.

XIX.—ECCLESTON HALL COLLIERY.

This colliery is situated two and a-quarter miles west of the town of St. Helens, and one and a-half miles north-east of Prescot. It is an old colliery now being reopened by the Worsley Mesnes Colliery Company, of Wigan. The minerals are leased from Mr. Samuel Taylor, whose estate adjoins Knowsley-park, the property of the Earl of Derby.

Geological.—The geological features are interesting, the outcrop of the New Red sandstone lying about half-a-mile to the south of the shafts, which are sunk entirely through Middle coal measures. The Bunter series of New Red sandstone comprises—Upper Mottled sandstone, the Pebble beds, Lower Mottled sandstone. The Pebble beds, which are estimated to be 600 ft. in thickness, are largely developed in this locality, the sandstone, with its peculiar quartz pebbles, being much used for building purposes.

Several shafts appear to have been sunk on the Eccleston Hall Estate by former lessees of the minerals; two of these shafts, sunk to the Main delf, have been utilised by the present company, who, on commencing their operations, found them filled with water to the surface, and they subsequently found out after an immense volume of water had been lifted to the surface, that accumulations of water in the old workings of the Main delf and the Flaggy delf had been contended with, besides the ordinary feeders issuing from fissured sandstones in various parts of the two shafts, which are running at the present time; the water-lifting operations had, in fact, drained all the workings to the rise of the water-levels in the Main delf.

The north shaft, or No. 1, was 9 ft. diameter to the Main delf, 84 yards depth, and has been sunk 137 yards further, of the same size, to the Arley Mine or Little delf. No. 2 shaft is 60 yards, south of No. 1, and was sunk by the former lessees 84 yards and 10 ft. in diameter to the same delf; the present company have sunk this shaft 137 yards further, and 13 ft. in diameter, leaving the upper part to be stripped and re-lined at a future time.

Water Lifting.—The chief part of the work of clearing the shafts and old workings of accumulated water was performed by No. 2 winding engine of 70-horse power, by means of wrought iron barrels, one running in No. 2 shaft of 600 gals. capacity, the other in No. 1 shaft of 500 gallons capacity. The situation was well adapted to give the best results by this method, one barrel being raised in one shaft, while the second barrel descended in the other shaft. It is stated that during two months or more the quantity of water raised was about 550 gallons per minute, or one barrel of water raised and discharged per minute. And this was supplemented afterwards by an engine and pump of the Tangye type, placed on temporary bearings in each shaft, being moved down in stages as the water was lowered. No. 1 pump has one $14\frac{1}{2}$ in. cylinder, 2 ft. stroke, and an 8 in. double-acting plunger. No. 2 has a 16 in. cylinder, 2 ft. stroke, and 7 in. double-acting plunger.

In deepening the shafts from the Main delf considerable feeders were encountered, but the principal rush of water came off when the Rushey Park old workings were reached, which had been driven from a pair of shafts some distance away and sunk about sixty years ago; these workings, being much less extensive than those named above, were soon cleared of water. No feeders are found below the Rushey Park Mine. At the present time No. 2 pump is placed in a lodge room in the Rushey Park Mine, and forces a small quantity of water 80 yards up to a lodge room in the Main delf, where No. 1 pump is placed permanently, which forces water to the surface 84 yards through 6 in. rising mains. This engine is driven at a speed of forty-five revolutions per minute, delivering about 360 gallons per minute. These engines practically raise all the water that runs into the shafts at the present time. The accompanying sketch shows a side view of a tank or barrel of 500 gallons capacity for raising water, the barrel being filled automatically through the valves, A and B, when it drops into the water, and the contents are discharged at the top of the shaft through the same valves by means of the rod, D, and the lever, E. When the barrel is lowered upon the running jiddy the valve, A, is forced upwards by the rod D. The valves are about 20 in. diameter.

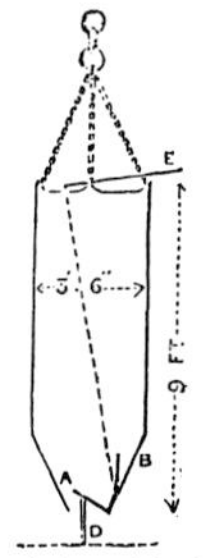

The coal seams sunk through in the Eccleston shafts are as follow:—

	Ft. in.	Thickness of coal. Ft. in.	Depth from surface. Yds.
The Sir John delf:—Coal		2 0	
Flaggy delf:—			
Coal	2 2		
Shale	1 2		
Coal	2 2		
		4 4	
Main delf:—			
Coal	2 6		
Clod	1 0		
Coal, with 9 in. poor in the middle	5 6	8 0	84
Rushey Park seam, good house coal now worked		4 6	164
Arley mine, good (all intact)		2 6	221

Winding.—The winding engine at the north or No. 1 shaft has two horizontal cylinders, 25 in. by 38 in. slide valves, and 11 ft. cylindrical drum. The south or No. 2 engine has two horizontal cylinders, 25 in. by 54 in., slide valves run on rollers, and 11 ft. drum. The engine-house is placed between the shafts and serves for both engines; owing to a depth of 3 to 4 yards of drift, the excavation for the foundations was heavy and the masonry, of considerable depth, consisted of bricks set in ordinary mortar and cement. The side walls of the house are 14 in. brickwork.

Hauling.—An engine placed on the surface has been adapted for underground haulage. It has two horizontal cylinders, 24 in. diameter, 2 ft. stroke. The reversing gear is moved by means of a large hand wheel and a pair of cog wheels.

Boilers.—Two Lancashire boilers, 30 ft. by $7\frac{1}{2}$ ft., supply steam at 70 lb. pressure to all engines, including the pumping engines in the shaft. There are four cross tubes in each flue; the boilers are fed by an injector with live steam.

The head gear at No. 2 shaft is $60\frac{1}{2}$ ft. above the surface, and the pit bank is 22 ft. above the surface, which gives ample height for screening arrangements.

Screens.—The accompanying figures represent side views of screens at Eccleston Hall Colliery:—

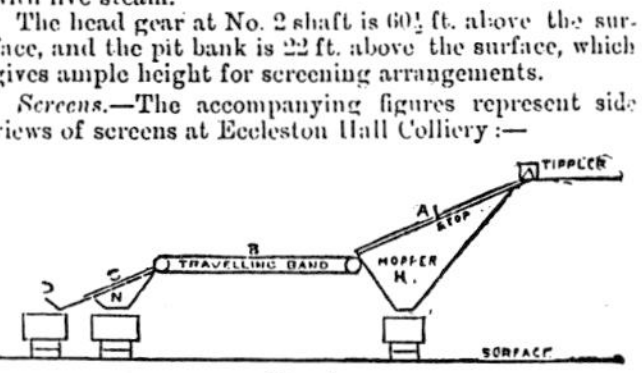

FIG. 1.

Fig. 1.—A is the large coal screen, fixed, with steel bars; the large coal falls upon the steel travelling band, B, 30 ft. long, 4 ft. wide; the plates are 6 in. wide, upon this band the coal is cleared of all impurities, and is then delivered on a second bar screen, separating a portion of the small coal as nuts, which fall into the hopper, N. At D a rising and falling shoot is provided. The slack hopper is at H. There is a door or stop at A which passes the coal through in regulated quantities. It is often seen that the coal falls upon the travelling bands in heaps, in which form it is impossible to clean out the foreign matter properly.

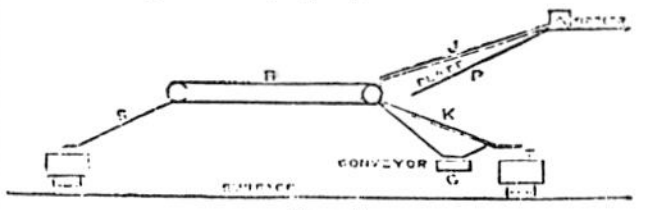

FIG. 2.

Fig. 2.—The large coal is treated on the jigging screen, J, made of wire network, 40 square feet in area, vibrated lengthways; it is then delivered upon the steel travelling band, 30 ft. by 40 ft., from whence it passes down the shoot, *s*, into trucks; this shoot has a movable end. The small coal that goes through the screen, J, drops upon the plate, P, which conveys it to the head of another jigging screen, K, with a reverse inclination, the area of wire network being about 24 square feet; the nuts pass over this screen into trucks at T, and the slack which passes through falls through the hopper upon a conveyor, G, which carries it to the trucks on a separate line of rails to that at T. This conveyor is 24 ft. long, 4 ft. wide. An engine with a 12 in. cylinder works the travelling bands, conveyor, and jigging screens by means of a line of shafting and spur gearing. M. E.

Rapidity of Kindling, and Influence of Eastern Coals on Boiler Preservation.—For lighting up and forcing the fires, Poronaï and Kelung coals are suitable, while bituminous and semi-bituminous coals of the Takasima class, though not so small as that coal, may be recommended for kindling, a necessary condition being that at least half the grate be covered with lumps. With coal containing a great deal of dust, a few logs of wood should be interspersed in the layer of coal, so as to avoid delay in getting up steam. The products given in Column 7 show generally what coals are to be preferred for rapid steaming. As is well known, the quantity of heat Q, employed for evaporation, depends upon several elements, being expressed by the formula:—$Q = u \times p \times c \times s$, in which u is the utilisation, c the calorific capacity, s the grate surface, and p the weight of the fuel in question. For a constant surface in the same vessel, the relative values of Column 4 are exactly proportional to the product $u \times c$, the quantity p remaining a very variable factor with the same kind of coal, as it depends considerably on the mean size of the lumps, the proportion of small and that of dust. For instance, half as much again Takasima coal may be burnt, if made into briquettes as in its natural state; but high speeds cannot long be maintained with inferior coals, on account of the rapid choking of the grate and the fatigue of firing, notwithstanding that large lumps be used. In this connection steamers whose firegrates may be temporarily enlarged have a great advantage. Forced draught is not suitable for either a pure coal with much dust, or for one which, though in large lumps, contains too much inert matter. The air under pressure pierces the layer of the first-named coal in places, and carries the small up the stack, while it leads to too rapid choking of the grate with the second. With coals like Takasima the stokehold may be ventilated with-

EXCERPT FROM THE COLLIERY GUARDIAN (Wigan Reference Library)

FLORIDA COLLIERY

This colliery was situated off Clipsley Lane and Church Road, Haydock. The colliery mined the Florida coal in the eighteenth century. All the coal from this colliery was transported on the Sankey Canal.

FRODSHAM COLLIERY

This was a small colliery in the St.Helens area that was mentioned in the 1894 Report as being under the ownership of the Liverpool and St.Helens Brick and Coal Co. with a workforce of 70 people.

GARSWOOD COLLIERY

The colliery was situated at Stanley Bank, Haydock, on the Old Garswood Hall Estate. It was referred to in the Inspector's Reports in the 1860's and 70's when it was owned by Bromilow and Co.

The production in the 1860's was reported to be 130,000 tons per year.

From *'THE REPORT OF THE MINES INSPECTOR'.*
16th February 1858.

Edward McLoughlin aged 30 years, the hooker-on at the colliery was killed falling into the pit from the Rushy Park mouthing to the Little Delf Mine.

The colliery was very close to the Laffak Colliery and at some time they were connected, the men descending to the workings of the Laffak Colliery by way of the Garswood Colliery. The boundaries of Lord Gerard's leases and those of the Laffak Colliery met in the area.

On the 14th. May 1866, twelve men and boys were killed in an explosion of firedamp and on the 20th. August 1867, a further fourteen lives were lost from the same cause.

GARSWOOD PARK COLLIERY

From the *'COLLIERY GUARDIAN'.*
26th. January 1861.
BREACH OF THE RULES

Bartholemew Hooton was charged before the St. Helens Petty Sessions with a breach of Rule No. 44, neglecting to inspect a safety lamp. He pleaded not guilty and was defended by Mr. Ward. The prosecution said that by his act, an explosion of gas had taken place and burnt James Marsh. He was found guilty and sentenced to fourteen days in jail.

COLLIERY HEADING OF WAYBILL (Mr. J. Atherton)

From *'THE WIGAN EXAMINER'.*
30th. November 1863.
OVERWINDING.

Two men were drawn up with great force but the engineer checked the cage in time to save them. The underlooker and a collier were in the cage but it was stopped before it hit the headgear. The accident was caused by the steam brake failing and there can be no blame to the engineer.

GERARDS BRIDGE COLLIERY

The colliery was situated at the side of College Street near the canal. This colliery appeared in 1805 as 'Gerrotts Bridge', and again in 1829 in connection with the railways. In the late 1830's the colliery was owned by Speakman Caldwell and Co. The 1860's must have been quite profitable for the colliery, when it was raising 50,000 tons of coal per year, all transported by railway. The colliery closed in the 1870's. It last appeared in the 'Inspector's Report' for 1873, when it was owned by William Middlehurst.

From *'THE REPORT OF THE INSPECTOR OF MINES'.*
8th. June 1851.

T. Cartwright was killed by falling out of a tub while ascending the shaft.

From *'THE WIGAN EXAMINER'.*
11th. August 1854.

At the Nelson Inn, there was an inquest on the body of Edward Hazelden aged 17 years who was badly burnt as a result of an explosion of firedamp at the pit. He died on the 12th. and a verdict of 'accidental death' was recorded with the cause of the explosion put down to the use of a naked candle.

From *'THE COLLIERY GUARDIAN'*
29th. May 1858.
SMOKING IN THE PIT.

At St.Helens Petty Sessions on Tuesday last, Thomas Cunliffe a drawer at the pit was charged with a breach of the Special Rule No. 9, smoking in the Rushy Park pit on the 13th. inst. Lamps were exclusively used in the mine and he had unlocked his lamp. He was sentenced to six weeks imprisonment at Kirkdale Prison.

From *'THE PRESCOT REPORTER'.*
25th. February 1860.
COLLIERS MARCH.

It is reported that the colliers do not know what to do in the strike. They claim that they are being paid 1854 wages. The masters will not give way and many men are at work. On Thursday morning there was a meeting from which two to three hundred men marched to Haydock to seek the support of the colliers there. It was resolved that the strike would continue.

On 10th. February, the same paper reported that the strike was terminated.

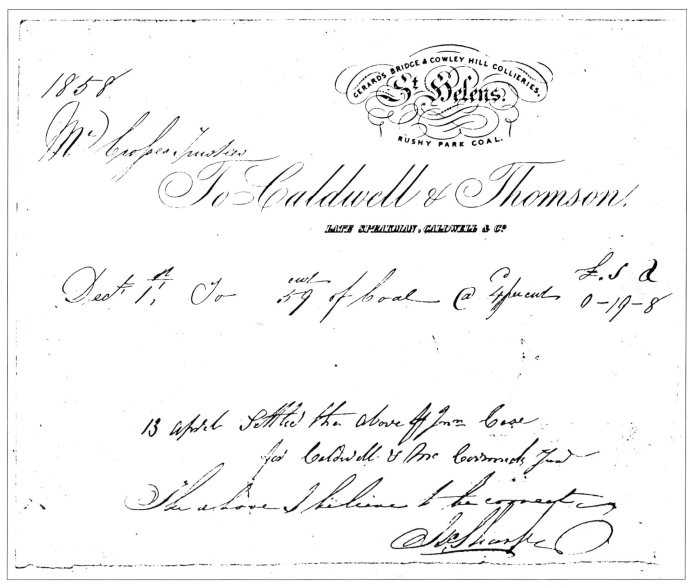

COAL DECLARATION DATED 1861 (Mr. J. Atherton)

From 'THE ST.HELENS NEWSPAPER'
11th. October 1862.

Some boys said that they had seen a youth fall down an old coal pit near Gerards Bridge. Every effort was made and a winding machine was placed over the shaft. A man went down 38 yards and found a hungry dog that had lived for a number of days on the carcasses of it's more unfortunate friends that had fallen down the shaft.

The children were severely admonished by the police.

Very little information and even fewer records remain of the coal owners in the town but Caldwell Thompson owned this colliery.

GILLARS GREEN COLLIERY

The colliery was situated on Burrows Lane, opposite Gillars Lane. There was a colliery in that area between 1753 and 1765, worked by the local squire, Mr.B.T.Eccleston. Another colliery is recorded in that area in the 1840's and 1850's and this colliery had links with the railways. The 'Inspector's Reports' of 1873 show a colliery being sunk there, but records show it was closed in 1883.

COLLIERY HEADING OF WAYBILL (Mr. J. Atherton)

From *'THE ST.HELENS STANDARD'*.
13th. February 1875.

There was a serious accident at the colliery on Monday morning when John Alexander Brophy aged 23 years lost his life.

He and his brother were being drawn up the shaft and came to within twenty yards of the top when it's progress was suddenly checked causing the cage to be knocked against the side of the shaft and he was thrown out. He fell forty five yards down the shaft. He died half an hour later.

GIN LANE COLLIERY

It was referred to in the 1850 Report to be under the ownership of David Bromilow and Co. and was in Parr, St.Helens.

GLADE HILL COLLIERY

The colliery was situated at the bottom of Islands Brow. A colliery at Glade Hill was mentioned in the 1790's, and was worked by James Orrell of Blackbrook up to the 1820's. It next appeared in the 'Inspector's Reports' for 1850 and 1855, but not later than the 1870's. At that time it was owned by John and Thomas Johnson, who later became soap manufacturers.

COLLIERS MINE 1926 (Mr. Simm)

COAL DECLARATION DATED 1861 (Mr. J. Atherton)

From *'THE REPORT OF THE MINES INSPECTOR'*.
18th. March 1859.

It is reported that George Lloyd aged 59 years, a furnaceman was found dead in the return way.

From *'THE REPORT OF THE MINES INSPECTOR'*.
19th. April 1856.

Mr.Peter Higson, the Mines Inspector for the area, reported that a collier neglected to get down the stratum which lies between the Higher Delf Mine and the roof according to instructions, which had been specially given to him by the Underlooker. The collier was killed in consequence. The parting stratum which must be removed immediately after the coal. In order to remedy this evil, the description of the labour should be paid for separate from working the coal, as colliers are in the habit of allowing it to stand, sometimes on props, but frequently without any support in order to make the largest amount of wages, until the daywagemen arrive to do the job. The labour had, however, to be performed during the following shift but this they do not consider.

During the Strike of 1926, many colliers sunk their own 'private' mines. The colliers of Glade Hill were no exception.

GREENGATE COLLIERY

The colliery was situated by Elephant Lane. This colliery was first mentioned in 1869, when coal was being sold by W. Walmesley and Co. In the Inspector's Report of 1873, the colliery had four pits, all drifts, and were worked by John Cross and Co. Ltd. He was the partner of W.J. Menzies of Greenbank Alkali Works. The colliery later appeared in the ownership of the Greengate Brick and

Tile Co, when there were only eighteen men working there. The colliery closed in 1915.

This colliery was owned by the Greengate Alkali Company and had a close connection with the chemical industry in the town.

From *'THE REPORT OF THE MINES INSPECTOR'*.
10th. January 1873.

Michael McDermott aged 16 years, a labourer, was killed by an explosion of powder left by sinkers in a hut.

GREEN LANE COLLIERY

This colliery was situated at the side of Dentons Green Lane near Duke Street. The colliery was opened in 1845, being sunk by Robert Whyte, but was only worked for a few years, closing in 1848.

HALSNEAD COLLIERY

The colliery was in Whiston and appears in the Inspector's Reports in 1850 as being owned by Richard Willis. In 1855 it was owned by Lee, Williams and Pugh. The colliery then disappeared from the Reports for a number of years but it appeared again in 1888 under the name of the Halsnead Colliery Co., Whiston, Prescot. It was reported as closing in 1895.

HARDSHAW COLLIERY

Coal had been mined in the Hardshaw district since the eighteenth century and the area was covered with small collieries at this time. There were several owners, Reverend Baldwin, W.Cotham and West and Co.

In the nineteenth century the business of the colliery was documented in the 'Hardshaw Colliery Letter Book' (1805-1815.) It was owned

by the Greenall family, the local brewers, and Joseph Churton, a local doctor. The colliery was mentioned in the 1855 'Inspector's Report' when John Middlehurst is recorded as the owner. It produced about 9,000 tons of coal a year, which was sold locally. The colliery closed in 1867.

From *'THE REPORT OF THE MINES INSPECTOR'*.
26th. June 1862.

Bennett Carter aged 31 years, a collier, was killed by a fall of roof.

There are many deaths of colliers, drawers and datallers that are recorded in the Inspectors Reports by these simple words.

HAYDOCK COLLIERIES

This was the collective term for all Richard Evans's Collieries situated in Haydock, Ashton, Parr and Golborne but there was a Haydock Colliery which was situated north and south of Clipsley

Lane and Church Road, Haydock. Over a period of 100 years, this colliery, comprised of various shafts sunk and used at different times. It was initially worked by the Legh Family and after 1833 by Turner and Evans. Later this Company became Richard Evans & Co. The shafts were named, No.1 Pit, No.2 Pit, Engine Pit, Legh Pit, King Pit, Ellen Pit, Queen Pit, Chelsea Pit and Princess Pit.

The Haydock Collieries were a large group that covered the whole St. Helens area. They were the result of

MR. RICHARD EVANS FROM ROMANCE OF COAL

the investment by the Evans family of Haydock and started by Mr. Richard Evans who came to the area in 1833 from London where he had previously been a successful publisher in Paternoster Square.

John Lawson Kennedy, the Commissioner appointed by Parliament to enquire into the conditions of 'Children Working in Coalmines' visited Haydock in 1841.

Evidence given to the Commission by DINAH BRADBURY, waggoner at Mr. Evans Colliery at Haydock. May 19th. 1841.

"What age are you?"

"I cannot tell you, to tell the truth, but I think I am between 18 and 19 years old".

"You are a drawer I believe?"

"Yes, I am; I draw for two men, but one of them has hurt himself, so I am out soon today."

"Do you use the belt and chain?"

"No, we don't need 'em, we have rails laid in these pits; the rails are laid up to every man's place, and we waggon them".

"What length of hours do you work?"

"I go down between four and five o'clock in the morning, and I come up between five and six in the evening."

"Do you ever work at night?

"No, we never work at night in these pits".

"Have you many small children in these pits?"

"Oh yes, a great deal".

"What time do you have for meals?"

"We generally stop to have meals when we have time, and generally find time."

At this point in the proceedings Dinah burst out:-

"At what age do you you intend to turn us out of the pit? Put me down 15 years old. I should like to be turned out."

"Do you then not like your present employment?"

"No. I don't, and I would not go down if I could get anything else to do".

EXCERPT FROM JOHN LAWSON KENNEDY'S REPORT (SMM)

In Mr. Kennedy's report for the whole of Lancashire, the only person that made an outburst like this was Dinah. Does this say something about the character of 'Yickers'?

John Lawson Kennedy added a footnote to this evidence which is very illuminating about the attitude of Richard Evans to his workers.

[*"Mr. Evans' colliery, in which 1000 hands are employed, is beautifully situated in the neighbourhood of Newton-le-Willows. Great credit is due to this gentleman for the pains he is taking to ameliorate the condition of the colliers in his employ. There is a day school attached to the premises, and on the day I was there 70 children were being educated — there would be nearly an equal number of boys and girls; the school is exceedingly neat and the children very orderly and clean. This school-room is attended by 200 children and young persons on Sunday, and as many of the workpeople are Methodists Mr Evans allows their clergy to preach in the school-room; all sects are allowed to preach there if they think fit. The Sunday-school is very well conducted, and the ladies of the family take a a great interest in its success. Mr Evans had built a row of 30 cottages. Each cottage contained four rooms, and to each is attached a small garden of nearly a rood of ground; I was glad to see many of the colliers busy working in their garden at the time I was there; pigsties were also built about 20 yards from the house, a good sign of the condition of the colliers. I went through many of the houses, and found them with a few exceptions only, exceedingly neat, tidy and well cleaned several were remarkably nicely kept, and well stocked with furniture. The privies are detached from the cottages, and appeared tolerably clean. The condition the colliers in Haydock contrast most favourably with those of Wigan, Pemberton, Orrell, Blackrod and Aspull, who are, without exception, the most degraded and wretched class of beings which had ever fallen under my notice. There seems nothing to which this can be attributed but the attention of a resident master"]*

EXCERPT FROM JOHN LAWSON KENNEDY'S REPORT (SMM)

From *'THE REPORT OF THE MINES INSPECTOR'.*
7th. December 1850.

Four men, who are not named, were killed in an explosion of firedamp in the Rushy Park Mine. The Inspector went on to comment that in this district since 21st. November thirty three explosions have occurred resulting in the loss of fifty three lives. Of these, the accident at Haydock, where four lives were lost when the whole pit swept by the blast was occasioned by an accumulation of gas formed by propping open an air door.

The first Government Inspectors with power to go underground, were appointed and the above extract appears in their first Report in 1850.

From *'THE REPORT OF THE MINES INSPECTOR'.*
27th. July 1852.

An explosion took place in the Florida Mine workings in the Rock Pit in the top part of the dip heading or downbrow which was in advance of the air and had been standing for some time. There being water in the bottom of it, some hay had been placed across the top to prevent the horses getting drowned, which interfered with the free ventilation of the gas and an accumulation took place at the back of the hay. A boy behaving incautiously, crept through with a naked candle and an explosion took place which burnt him to death.

From *'THE REPORT OF THE MINES INSPECTOR'.*
16th. August 1855.

Two men named Burrows and Simm were suffocated by afterdamp from an explosion of firedamp in No.1 Florida Pit, when a man looking for a place to stow rubbish climbed into some old workings with a naked light and there being firedamp present it exploded. The person who lit it escaped but two persons were suffocated by the afterdamp.

From *'THE REPORT OF THE MINES INSPECTOR'.*
4th. October 1856.

Thomas Melling was run over in the shunt of the waggon road by a waggon filled with coals and killed.

From *'THE REPORT OF THE MINES INSPECTOR'.*
15th. November 1863.

THE COLLIERY SCHOOL (Mr. Bond)

Thomas Pimblett aged 67 years, a dataller, was killed as he was crossing the eye of the pit when the descending cage stuck him on the head. He had not passed this way for some time and there was a road along which he should have travelled. The deceased undoubtedly contributed to his own fate.

From **'THE WIGAN OBSERVER'**
22nd. January 1864.

The inquest into the death of Margaret Knowles, a labourer, was held at the Waggon and Horses, which was John Greenall's house, on Friday. She was 17 years old and employed at the No 1 pit when she and two other girls were pushing two full waggons when she slipped on a sleeper and fell over. Several waggons passed over her and she was crushed. She died on the 13th.

She was a well conducted and good girl who supported her mother since her father was crushed in the pit about fifteen weeks ago and died. Her sister is an imbecile and cannot work. Verdict, 'accidental death'.

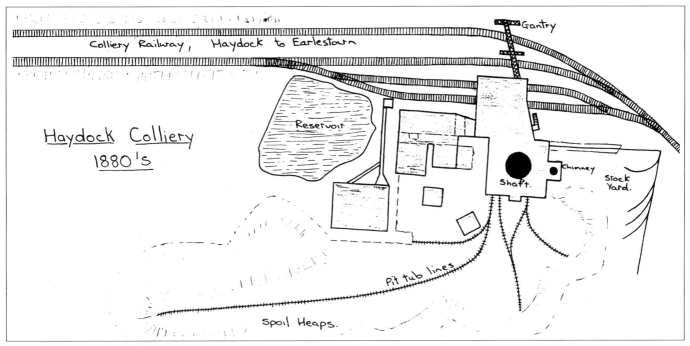

SURFACE PLAN OF THE COLLIERY (Mr. Simm)

HAYDOCK, ASHTON, EDGE GREEN, PARR, AND GOLBORNE COLLIERIES.

DUTIES OF THE UNDERLOOKERS ENGAGED AT THESE PITS.

1.—The Underlooker shall have the daily supervision and responsible charge of the Pit, under the direction of the Manager.

2.—To enter the Pit Daily at 5.45 a.m. and to leave at 3.45 p.m.

3.—To meet Night Firemen at the Pit each night at 5.45 p m.

4.—To see the General and Special Rules are duly observed, and to suspend any one infringing any Rule, and to order him out of the Pit, and immediately report the non-observance of the same to the Manager; to receive the Reports of the Firemen, and daily advise with and instruct them. To give immediate attention to any complaint, and inspect personally such part of the Pit as may be reported unsafe, or need his attention thereto, and to remedy any defect.

5—He shall immediately send notice of any Accident to the Manager.

6.—Not to leave the Pit during working hours without written permission from the Manager.

7.—To adjust the Barometer and Thermometer daily, and register their indications, and when any unusual fall of the Barometer has taken place, to caution Firemen, Furnacemen, and Shot-lighters.

8.—To visit and examine every working place in the Pit at least once every other day, and order all Props, Chocks, Timber, Stores, and other material, from the Manager, and see them sent into the districts where needed, and to report any deficient supply to the Manager.

9.—To measure and examine the air currents daily, and if there be any deficiency in the ventilation, to take proper steps for having it remedied, also from time to time to travel the returns and all accessible parts of the Mine, examining all Doors, Stoppings, Air Crossings, and Regulators, and to see that they are kept in good order.

10.—To see that all Entrances to any place not in actual course of working and extension, are properly fenced across the whole width of such Entrance, so as to prevent persons inadvertently entering the same

11.—To see that the Stations for re-lighting Lamps are well attended to, and that the person in charge keep the Box locked, to prevent any person having access to the same

12.—Before "holing" into any place not working to use additional caution and to carry out General Rule 9.

13.—To provide Manholes, or places of refuge, in all Engine-planes, Jig-brows, Balance-brows, and Horse-roads, and to keep them constantly clear, as per General Rules 10, 11, and 12.

14.—To examine daily the Report-Books at the Mine, and see that the Reports are properly recorded therein.

NOTICE TO UNDERLOOKERS (Mr. Simm)

From 'THE ST.HELENS NEWSPAPER'
7th. January 1865.

On Thursday afternoon there was an accident at Haydock to James Whittle aged 22 years, a drawer, when he was killed on the spot and a collier named Robert Carr was crushed about the body when a portion of the roof fell on them in the Main Delf Mine where they were working. They were extracted from the debris and carried home. The deceased lived at Parr and had been married only three months

From 'THE WIGAN OBSERVER'.
19th. February 1865.
STRIKE.

It is reported that Evans Colliers are on strike and those at Gerards Bridge also. Fifteen hundred men are out and the management want them to work twelve hours a day when the custom in the district is nine hours.

The Haydock Colliery was one of the first in the village and a surface plan of

NOTICE OF EXCURSION TO BLACKPOOL (Mr. Simm)

the colliery is seen on the previous page.

According to the 'Coal Mines Regulation Act' notices had to be put up at the pit head detailing the duties of the work people.

Blackpool was the favourite place for a day out for miners and their families all over Lancashire. Haydock was no exception.

Times were hard in the depression years and colliers did not earn a great deal, even if they could get work.

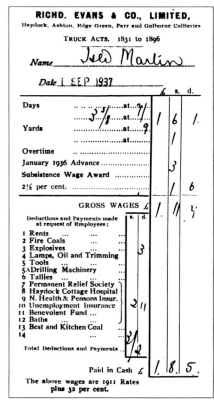

PAY SLIP FROM RICHARD EVANS & CO. (Mr. Simm)

HOLLIN HEY COLLIERY

This colliery was situated at the side of Old Garswood Road. Little is known of this colliery only that it was owned by James Gorner & Sons, its manpower was 19, and it closed in 1934.

The coal seams outcropped in this area and there were several 'outcrop' mines dug by colliers in the 1921 and 1926 strikes.

OUTCROP MINE IN 1921 STRIKE (Mrs. Morris)

The photograph is of such a mine that was dug by Richard Brown in the 1921 strike. In the photograph are three of the Marsh family and Tom Maudsley. The man in the cap is not named. All the men lived in Blackbrook, Haydock

KING COLLIERY

King, Queen, Legh and Princess pits were situated close together opposite the offices of Richard Evans and Co. in Haydock. King and Queen pit were producing coal before 1833, the latter having been called Ellen pit.

Legh pit was sunk in 1873 when the shafts were mentioned separately in the 'Inspectors Report'. In 1894 Legh pit employed 250 people, Queen pit 300, and Princess pit 400. All the shafts were abandoned in the early part of this century. Princess was the last to close in 1920.

LAFFAK COLLIERY

The colliery was situated in Newlyn and Bodmin Groves. The Legh Family of Lyme were mining in that area in the 1760's, when it was sometimes referred to as 'Laffog'. In the 1840's, John and Thomas Johnson were the owners of Laffak, with the colliery appearing in the 1850 and 1855 'Inspector's Reports' but not in any Report later than the 1870's. Production was reported to be 60,000 tons per year in 1862.

From *'THE WIGAN EXAMINER'.*
16th. March 1855.
John Fairclough, a boy, took the hoppet down the pit and signalled to descend when he fell out and was killed. The inquest was held at the Royal Arms at Parr with the attendance of the Government Inspector when a verdict of 'accidental death' was returned.

On 11th. March 1855, the Inspector of Mines reported that the horsekeeper

KING COLLIERY (Mr. Simm)

had drowned in the water tank at the bottom of the pit.

From ***'THE ST.HELENS INTELLIGENCER'.***
13th. September 1856.

John Sefton and Joseph Salton were killed in a cage accident at the colliery when Sefton was drawn over the pulley at the top of the headgear and Salton jumped and fell down the pit.

At the inquest at the Wellington Hotel it was disclosed that several men were injured and the inquest was adjourned until the bolts that held the cage could be produced.

At the resumed inquest Thomas and John Johnson, the proprietors of the colliery, were summoned by the Government Inspector, Mr. Peter Higson, for not observing the Rules 18 and 19 Vict. about the brake on the engine when two men lost their lives. The charge was withdrawn and Mr. Greenough, the underlooker at the colliery, pleaded guilty to the offence and was fined £2 with 12/4d. costs.

From ***'THE PRESCOT REPORTER.'***
14th. September 1861.

John Horsley and Joseph Making, both colliers, were summoned for taking the tops off their lamps in the mine and fined 20/- and 5/6d. costs for the former and 25/- and 5/- costs for the latter.

From ***'THE ST.HELENS NEWSPAPER AND ADVERTISER'.***
24th. September 1867.
FATAL ACCIDENT AT LAFFAK COLLIERY.

On Tuesday an accident occurred at the colliery in which a young man about 24 years of age named William Pearce had his shoulder dislocated.

He was working in the mine when a portion of the roof fell on him. Another account of the matter is that, contrary to the Rules, he was riding on one of the boxes that was passing down the brow and by some means caught his shoulder against the roof.

With the assistance of some men he was brought out of the pit, placed in a cart, and taken home to Gerards Bridge. The services of Dr. Gaskell were obtained and he is now recovering.

The change of ownership of a colliery was quite common and when they came up for sale, an inventory usually appeared in the sale notice.

MONDAY and TUESDAY, the 3rd and 4th days of April, 1871.

IN LIQUIDATION.

LAFFAK COLLIERY, NEAR ST. HELENS.

Sale of the remaining plant, machinery, and buildings, &c., at the above colliery.

MESSRS. LAMB AND SONS, beg to intimate that they have been favoured with instructions to SELL BY AUCTION, on Monday and Tuesday, at twelve o'clock each day prompt, at the above colliery, the remaining plant, machinery, and buildings, &c., comprising one high-pressure vertical winding and pumping engine, 34-inch cylinder, 5ft stroke, fly-wheel 16ft diam., drum 8ft diam., with verticals for flat rope 16ft diam., and pumping driving wheel on shaft 8ft diam. by 12in pitch (by R. Dalglish, St. Helens); two egg-ended boilers, each 30ft long by 6ft 6in by ⅜in, with 2 6-in valves, and two 3-in valves, and all other mountings complete; one table engine, 12-in cylinder, 3ft stroke, with 6ft pumping wheel and pinion, eccentric, &c.; one cast iron pendulum and L. leg, with balance weights, pedestals, bolts, &c, complete; high pressure horizontal donkey engine, 8-in cylinder, 15-in stroke, with 4-in pump, 12-in stroke, pipes and gearing complete; one egg-ended boiler, 22ft long by 4ft by ⅜in, with 2 safety valves, stop valve, water gauge, taps, furnace and fire-bars complete; one high-pressure vertical engine, 12-in cylinder, 2ft 7½-in stroke, with feed pump, governor balls, and gearing complete (by George Scott, St. Helens); one cast iron drum, 6ft diam., 4ft long, with spur gearing shafts, pedestals, wall plates, and fitted with wrought iron break gear; winding drum, 3ft diam., 4ft long, with spur and break gearing attached; several engine beds of ashlar stone, wrought iron gasometer, with cast iron pillars and pulleys; wrought iron water bucket, 4ft 6in by 3ft 6in by 2ft 9in, with coupling chains and gearing complete; two head gear pulleys, each 12ft diam., for flat ropes, with pedestals and wrought iron centre bolts, &c.; pitchpine head gear and stageing; double deck cages, with coupling chains; about 80 tons of double headed, flange and bridge rails; cast iron tiplers, with wrought iron gearing; timber doors, &c.; 12 railway coal wagons; 220 coal boxes or tubs, to hold 7cwt; about 200 yards of flexible air tubeing, equal to new; wrought iron shafting, circular saw bench, fitted complete with gearing strap, pulleys, straps, adjusting slide boxes, &c; about 10 tons of cast iron incline and jigger pulleys and posts, round steel and flat wire ropes; quantity of signal wire, railway chairs, pitchpine guide rods, wrought and cast iron brow-plates, Norway propwood, cast iron crossings, pine logs, gas piping, wrought iron cisterns, leather strapping, stocks, taps, and dies; 144 Davy lamps, lamp bottoms, miners' dial and theodalite, oil cisterns; one pair of smiths' portable bellows, two iron water tubs, and 2 56lb weights attached; smiths' anvil, swage block and stand, cast iron block, wood benches, and a various assortment of smiths tools, quantity of new files, lot of nails and bolts, one pillar drilling machine, with pulleys, bits, &c., complete.

OFFICE FIXTURES, &c., include 2 patent fire-proof safes, by "Milner," writing desk, spring time-pieces, chimney glass, letter-press, Windsor chairs, excellent weather glass, fenders and fire-irons, &c., &c.

HORSES, CARTS, FARM IMPLEMENTS, &c.—One grey mare, "Fanny," 15 hands 1in. high, 9 years old, suitable for either saddle or harness, one draught horse, 16 hands 2in high, aged, three strong pit ponies, three stacks of well grown meadow hay, set of brass mounted harness, excellent Whitechapel, broad-wheeled carts, set of cart gears, leading gears, ploughing chains, night halters, &c.

The brick buildings forming stables, engine and boiler houses, lamp-house, and fitting shop, which are supported with strong pine principals and spars covered with blue slates, and all other loose material.

Catalogues will shortly be ready, and may be had at the Auctioneers, or will be forwarded on application, and any other information may be obtained from Messrs LAMB AND SONS, practical auctioneers, valuers, arbitrators, and general salesmen, contractors of plant, machinery, farm stock, estates, horses, carriages, silver plate, &c., (established nearly half a century) offices, King's chambers, 29, King-street, Wigan.

SALE NOTICE OF THE COLLIERY IN 1871 (Mr. Dobson)

LAFFAK-GARSWOOD COLLIERY

The colliery is mentioned in the Inspector's Reports for 1869 and 1873 as being owned by Bromilow and Co. It was situated in Parr.

LEA GREEN COLLIERY

The colliery was situated on Lowefield Lane and was probably sunk in the 1870's by James Radley. The history of the colliery is in two parts, the colliery is mentioned in the 1888 'Inspector's Report', as being owned by Mrs. F.P. Radley, the widow of James Radley.

The 1894 Report shows the colliery under the ownership of the Sutton Heath and Lea Green Collieries Ltd., employing about 450 work people. The Report also shows Lea Green new pits, employing approximately 100 men. It is possible that this colliery was just being sunk.

The colliery was profitable this century and had a reputation for high quality coal. It closed in August 1964. In that year it produced 200,000 tons of coal and employed 600 men.

From ***'THE REPORT OF THE MINES INSPECTORS'.***
5th. January 1886.

George Parr aged 45 years, the hooker-on at the colliery. It was stated at the inquest that the deceased had been struck on the head by a bolt falling down the shaft but a Doctor said that this had nothing to do with his death.

From ***'THE REPORT OF THE MINES INSPECTORS'.***
17th. January 1887.

William Lunt aged 53 years a stoneman was killed. He was very deaf and after lighting a shot and going to a safe place he appears to have heard the shot and returned to the place just as the shot went off. He was struck by stones from the blast.

From ***'THE REPORT OF THE MINES INSPECTORS'.***
4th. September 1890.

Thomas Hitchen aged 14 years, a pony driver was killed at 7.15 am in the 2nd. hour of the shift. He was working in front of a full gang of tubs and on reaching the shaft siding he lent down to unhook the pony but before he could get up he was jammed against some tubs in front. The accident was due to the excessive speed at which the ponies were driven.

From ***'THE REPORT OF THE MINES INSPECTORS'.***
14th. August 1895.

Peter Malone, a collier aged 40 years, was killed at 3.30 am. in the 8th. hour of the shift. The fireman lit a fuse without sufficiently examining the place which caused the gas at the face to explode causing injury to him and the deceased who died on the 20th. The brattice at the time was six feet from the face and the gas collected at the bottom.

From 'THE REPORT OF THE MINES INSPECTORS'.

8th. May 1896.

William Jones aged 25 years a collier, was in the act of lifting a box onto the rails he slipped backwards with his hand coming into contact with the rails. He died a week later from inflammation of the heart set up by ruptured muscles in his arm. The jury followed the medical evidence.

From 'THE REPORT OF THE MINES INSPECTORS'.

10th. December 1896.

Sydney Borrows aged 40 years a metalman was killed. A fireman from another district went to borrow a battery and it appears that he assisted in firing a shot. He fired the shot before the deceased had left the working place. He said that he did not know anyone else was there except the fireman who had gone to connect the wires and on seeing him return, he fired the shot without asking if there was anyone else there. The jury found both firemen guilty of great negligence.

From 'THE REPORT OF THE MINES INSPECTORS'.

7th. May 1902.

James Stephens aged 40 years, a stoker,

HEADGEARS OF THE COLLIERY (BC)

was killed when the blow-off pipe in front of the boiler burst, causing steam to escape. He was scalded and died on the 14th.

The water put on to cool the washers appears to have had a bad effect on the blow-out valve and loosened it when it was corroded. An inspection should have found this.

From 'THE REPORT OF THE MINES INSPECTORS'.

17th. June 1911.

Three labourers were killed at the Queen pit. John Duffy aged 42 years, Joseph Armstong aged 36 years, and Stephen Kelley

aged 55 years.

The accident occurred when they entered a wooden cabin at the pit top to take their dinner. The cabin toppled over and fell fifteen feet, owing to the fact that the plank on which it was resting had been sawn through during structural alterations.

From 'THE REPORT OF THE MINES INSPECTORS'.

9th. December 1912.

Thomas Regan aged 29 years, a contractor, was taking out bars, with others, to make the road higher. They were told to set timber before loosening any bars. . They knocked out a prop and attempted to draw the bar with a Sylvester. Failing to do this, Regan was using a pick to loosen the end of the bar when the roof fell on him. No temporary supports had been set.

From 'THE ST.HELENS REPORTER'.

20th. April 1926.

THATTO HEATH.

Collier's Death.

The mystery of a St.Helens mineworkers death was examined at the inquest by Mr Brighouse. The inquest was on John Prescott, of Owen Street, Thatto Heath, who was discovered dead in the Lea Green colliery, his body being three yards from a horizontal haulage wheel.

Underground photographs are rare. This one was taken in the 1950's.

The Haydock Colliery locomotives

COLLIERS UNDERGROUND (Mr. Simm)

THE BELLEROPHON LEAVING LEA GREEN COLLIERY 1966 (Mr. Simm)

have caused great interest to locomotive societies. The most famous one is the Bellerophon. It is seen here being removed from the colliery where it finished it's working life.

LEGH COLLIERY

This was one of the Haydock Collieries and was close to King, Queen and Princess pits.

This was one of the Richard Evans Collieries in Haydock and in the records the spelling varies. Lee, Lea and Leigh are all recorded but Legh is correct.

Following the Hartley Colliery Disaster in 1862 all collieries had to have two shafts, one the upcast or furnace shaft and the other the downcast shaft which wound the men and materials. Legh pit was the upcast

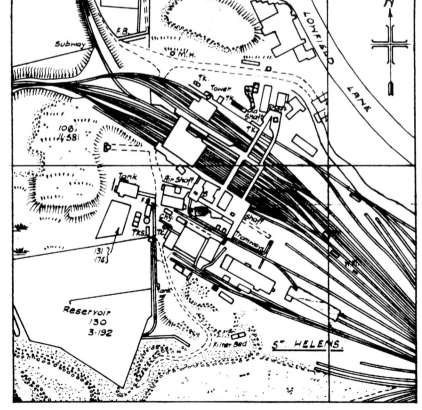

SURFACE PLAN OF THE COLLIERY

HAYDOCK COLLIERIES (Mr. Simm)

LYME COLLIERY

The colliery was situated between Earlestown and Haydock, near Lyme Street and was owned by Evans and Co. up to nationalisation in 1947.

Sinking was started in 1876 and reached 110 yards but the pumps of the time could not keep the shaft free from water since a large feeder was encountered during the operations.

By 1912 the technology had improved and work was continued with the building of an extensive surface plant but the work was again suspended due to the World War.

Sinking was resumed in 1919 when the new technique of pumping concrete into the shaft wall to seal the feeder was used.

shaft for the Queen Colliery and was unusual as it was about a quarter of a mile away from the upcast shaft.

From *'THE WIGAN EXAMINER'.*
3rd. February 1866.
SERIOUS CHARGE OF UNLAWFUL WOUNDING.

On Monday a youth named Wedgwood who stands charged that on the 12th inst. did unlawfully wound Abraham Simm who worked at Legh pit belonging to Messrs Evans and Co. was brought before McCorquodale Esq. by Inspector Peters.

It appears that the two of them, at three o'clock on the afternoon of the day named, were at work in a portion of the workings at the top of the shunt brow and a quarrel took place between them in respect of a tub. After some angry words the prisoner walked off about two hundred yards and returned with a large hammer with which he dealt Simm a violent blow on the head, inflicting a dreadful wound and rendering him insensible.

He was picked up by a man named Travis who took him home where he was attended to by Dr. Twyford. It was found that he had a severe fracture of the skull through which a portion of his brain protruded. He lies in a very critical state. Application for bail was refused.

On the 10th. February, The Wigan Examiner reported that Abraham Simm had died and at the inquest into his death the coroner brought in a verdict of 'wilful murder'. Wedgwood was bound over to attend the next Liverpool Assizes to answer the charge.

LEGH PIT.

RAVENHEAD HIGHER DELF.

To nnage	1/1¾
Ya rds on face	8/-
Ya rds on end	3/9
Ri bbings	1/2 1/8 1/10

RAVENHEAD MAIN DELF.

Tonnage	10½d.
Yards on face	3/3
Yards on end	3/6
Ribbings	1/3

9 FEET MINE.

Tonnage	11½d.
Yards on face	4/8
Yards on end	5/8
Ribbings, 3yds. wide (see below)	2/-
Cutting top coal down, per yard	10d.
Colliers working in making out places	5/- per day
Drawers working in making out places	4/- ,,
Men to find explosives.	
Colliers' day wage	3/10 ,,
Drawers	3/6 ,,

PRICES NOT SUBJECT TO PERCENTAGES.

Payment for Ley above the seam over 4 in. thick, 1d. per ton extra, with an additional 1d. per ton for every 4 in.

Crabbing, or pushing-up on the dip of the mine, after the first 13 yards, 1d. per ton down to 26 yards, and an additional 1d. per ton for every 10 yards afterwards.

Long Drawing.—Where drawing exceeds 150 yards on level, 1d. per ton extra up to 200 yards, and 1d. per ton for every additional 50 yards.

Where drawing exceeds 100 yards up brow, 1d. per ton extra, and 1d. per ton for every additional 50 yards, over 100 yards.

Filling tanks with water, 3d, per small tank, and 6d. per large tank.

Filling and emptying boxes with dirt, 8d. per box, including drawing; if beyond drawing limit, 1d. per box extra; 4d. per box if filled only; emptied only 4d. per box.

Setting 7 ft. bars, 5d. per bar.

Setting prop chocks 4 ft. 6 in. square, filled with dirt, 3s. 6d. each, and prop chocks above 4 ft. 6 in. high to be paid in like proportion.

Drawing props 1d. per prop.

Half-end and face places to be paid, half-end and face prices.

Ribbings to be 3 yards wide, and to be paid 2s. per yard, and for 6 yards wide, 1d. per ton on field price; after this width pillar price. If the Company order the place to be driven between 3 and 5 yards, ribbing price to be paid. If men exceed 3 yards wide on their own account no yards to be paid.

WAGES FOR LEGH PIT IN THE RAVENHEAD HIGHER AND MAIN DELF AND THE NINE FEET MINE, 1888 (Mr. Simm)

Before the nationalization of the coal industry in 1947 the colliery was one of the Haydock Collieries owned by Richard Evans and Company.

There were three shafts in use Nos 1 and 2 being used for coal winding and No 3 shaft for pumping.

The No.1 shaft, the downcast shaft started in 1876, was widened from 16 feet to 18 feet to reach the Florida seam at a depth of 395 yards in 1922. It was again deepened in 1932 to the Trencherbone Seam at 547 yards.

The No. 2 shaft, the upcast shaft, was 18 feet in diameter and reached the Florida seams in 1922 and was deepened in 1932 to exploit the Trencherbone seam. In 1936 a new reinforced concrete headgear was erected for the No. 2 pit.

New screens were installed in 1923 and a new coal washery in 1926. In 1964, the year the colliery closed, it was producing 180,541 tons a year and employed 500 people

The No. 3 shaft was 16 feet in diameter and was first sunk in 1876 to 125 yards and was abandoned for the same reason as No 1 shaft. It was used as a pumping shaft to deal with the water from the Permo-Triassic sandstone which overlies the coal measures.

Coal was first wound at the colliery in 1922. Both No. 1 and No. 2 shafts are equipped with steam winders and two deck cages each deck three holding 12.3 cwts. capacity tubs.

GEOLOGICAL FEATURES.

The coalfield is bounded on the west by the Twenty Acre Fault, which separates the field from the Bold Colliery and on the east by the Boston Fault which separates it from Wood Pit. On the northern boundary is the Red Rock fault running in an east-west direction. The field is sub divided by the Downall Green Fault and the Hazel Grove Fault.

The workings in the area between the Twenty Acre and the Downall Green Faults reveal the existence of considerable minor faulting. The full dip of the seams is generally 1 in 4 to the south east.

H. M. S. WASHER (Mr. Simm)

LYME COLLIERY IN 1936 (Mr. Simm)

STEPPING OUT OF THE CAGE
(Mr. Armstrong)

THE ENDLESS HAULAGE TO THE SCREENS
(Mr. Armstrong)

left to right, Mr. Joe Corday, overman, Mr. Paddy Redmond, senior overman, Mr. Arthur Baines, undermanager, Mr. Lloyd Thompson, Manager, Mr. Bill Fairclough, undermanager, Mr. Harry Turner overman and Mr. Jimmy Hatton, chief engineer.

THE 1949 EXPLOSION.

For some weeks, work to seal off the No 1 pit, which was worked out, had been going on. The work was very hot due to heating and men employed in the task had been taken to hospital suffering from heat exhaustion.

At 5.45 on the morning of 16th. September 1949, just as the night shift was going off duty there was a terrific explosion which blew out a massive stopping constructed of sand and cement.

The Mines Rescue Team from Boothstown was summoned and a team of five men went down the pit. Two of them lost their lives and another had a very lucky escape. Jimmy Page aged 34 years and Harold Clare aged 48 years were both overcome by gas and Herbert Evitts aged 44 years was found unconscious and dragged to safety by William Seth Parr aged 33 years.

Evitts received the British Empire Medal and Seth Parr the George Medal. The citation in the 'London Gazette' read:- *"In taking the decision to safety Parr was fully aware of the extreme risk ..... He had little oxygen left, and it was clear that, if he collapsed himself he could not rely on others helping him...".*

THE SURVIVORS WITH MATRON BONE (Mr. and Mrs. Pilling)

Disaster again visited Haydock when there was an explosion at the colliery on 26th. February 1930. The explosion killed five men and seriously injured twenty others. The death toll finally rose to thirteen. The efforts of Dr. Winifred Bridges, a young woman doctor, who went underground to tend to the injured, are still fondly remembered in Haydock today.

The 1st. January 1947 was a day that lives in the memories of many miners. This was the day that the long awaited nationalisation of the mines took effect. The nearest Sunday to that date was the 5th. January when there were celebrations at collieries all over the country.

The photograph was taken at the colliery on that day. The men are, from

NATIONALISATION 5th JANUARY 1947 (Mr. Redmond)

1949 EXPLOSION RESCUE TEAM (Mr. Redmond)

The photograph shows Mr. Jack Franklin, an electrician, Mr. Syd Smith, a deputy and Mr. Paddy Redmond coming down the steps with Mr. John Potter, an on-setter watching them. The reporter is not named.

Three men were decorated for their bravery in this incident, one of them a Haydock man.

Lives risked — all in the day's job
SIX WIN GEORGE MEDALS

By the KING'S Order the name of
Herbert Shaw,
Deputy, Lyme Colliery Lancashire,
was published in the London Gazette on
7 February, 1950,
as commended for brave conduct.
I am charged to record His Majesty's
high appreciation of the service rendered.

C. R. Attlee

Prime Minister and First Lord
of the Treasury

MR. SHAW'S CITATION AND LAUREL LEAF DOCUMENT (Mrs. Shaw)

WILLIAM SETH PARR AND HERBERT EVITTS (Mr. Redmond)

TELEPHONE:
BLACKFRIARS 8383

TELEGRAMS:
COALBOARD,
MANCHESTER

NATIONAL COAL BOARD
NORTH-WESTERN DIVISION,
LANCASHIRE HOUSE,
47, PETER STREET,
MANCHESTER, 2.

8th February, 1950.

Dear *W. Shaw*

It is with very great pleasure I have learned that His Majesty The King has been graciously pleased to award you a COMMENDATION in recognition of the courage and gallantry you displayed on the occasion of the underground explosion at Lyme Colliery on the 15th September, 1949.

The Divisional Board are delighted you have been honoured in this way, and take this opportunity of conveying to you their congratulations and best wishes.

May I add my own sincere congratulations to those already expressed and wish you every success in the future.

Yours sincerely,

W. J. DRUMMOND
Chairman.

H. Shaw Esq.,
86 Church Road,
HAYDOCK,
St. Helens,
Lancs.

LETTER FROM DRUMMOND, THE HEAD OF THE NATIONAL COAL BOARD (Mrs. Shaw)

MILL LANE COLLIERY

This was one of the Rainford collieries and referred to in the 1879 and 1888 Inspector's Reports. It was owned by the Mill Lane Mining Co. and did not produce coal but high quality fire clay.

MOSS HOUSE COLLIERY

This was at Rainford and referred to in the Inspector's reports of 1873 and 1888 as being owned by Thomas Baird and Co. There is no mention of the colliery after the 1890's.

From *'THE ST. HELENS STANDARD'*.
24th. February 1866.
THE EMPLOYMENT OF CHILDREN.

At an inquest into the death of a 12 year old girl, Ellen Hampson, who was killed at the Moss House Colliery, it was stated that she came from a large family and got a job at the pit to assist three other girls that were levelling slack as it was screened. They had to remove the trucks they were filling and replace them with empties.

She had been working for about an hour on the first morning. She went to an empty waggon and lifted the brake to allow it to run to the screen. As it approached the place where she wanted it, she tried to put on the brake but she was not strong enough and the buffer struck her in the chest and crushed her against a stationary waggon.

She was conveyed home, but lingered until Thursday. She had worked at the pit two years before her age and the Inspector, Mr. Higson thought it reckless conduct to set a girl to do this work.

The jury returned a verdict of accidental death and said that they regretted that such a young girl should be allowed to do such work.

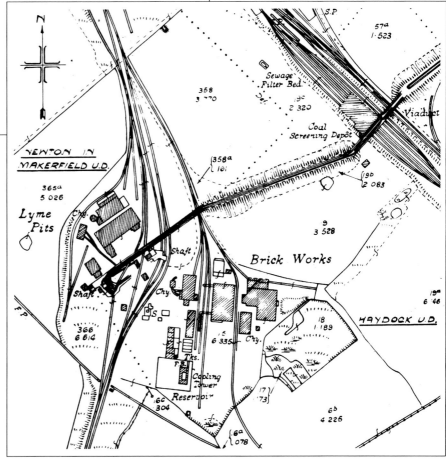

SURFACE PLAN OF LYME COLLIERY

NEW BOSTON COLLIERY

The colliery was situated south of Church Road, Haydock, opposite the Ram's Head Hotel. It was sunk about 1854 and became known locally as 'Ram Pit' although the official Ram pits were behind the Ram's Head Hotel on Kenyons Lane.

It is mentioned in the Inspector's Report of 1894 as employing 250 people. The colliery closed in 1907.

NEW BOSTON COLLIERY (Mr. Simm)

From *'THE REPORT OF THE INSPECTOR OF MINES'*.
28th. November 1862.

James Dearden aged 32 years, a collier was killed while stepping into the cage at the bottom of the shaft.

From *'THE REPORT OF THE INSPECTOR OF MINES'*.
28th. June 1883.

Thomas Twist aged 24 years, a collier, died after he was injured on the 9th. November by a fall of thin shell from the roof. His note at the inquest stated that there ought to have been more props set but there had been some difficulty in getting them from the store. More care on the part of the officials would have prevented this accident.

The worst accident at the colliery occurred on the 16th. July 1905 and resulted in the deaths of five men.

They were engaged, with others on a Sunday morning, in repairing a brow in the Ravenhead Delf. The road which was fifteen feet wide had been falling and under repair for about a week. They were putting a large baulk of timber across the road to complete the timbering when another fall occurred burying all five and two other men who escaped but were injured.

NUTGROVE COLLIERY

The colliery was situated at the end of Radley Street. This colliery appeared in the 'Inspector's Report' for 1873, being owned by James Radley, hence the name Radley Street. In the 1888 Report it was owned by his widow Mrs. F.P.Radley. It was reputed to have closed about that time.

From *'THE REPORT OF THE INSPECTOR OF MINES'*.
28th. March 1866.

It was reported that a man named Fenny, a stoker at the colliery, was killed when he fell into the winding gear of the engine.

From *'THE REPORT OF THE INSPECTOR OF MINES'*.

On the 2nd. November 1868, there was an underground fire at the colliery when William Naylor the 54 years old underlooker, John Campbell aged 21 years, a surveyor, and a waggoner, William Foster, aged 42 years, were suffocated from various vapours from the mine being given off by the fire.

OLD BOSTON COLLIERY

The colliery was situated north of Penny Lane, Haydock and was sunk in 1868 by Richard Evans and Co.. It was a profitable colliery for all it's life and at it's peak employed 800 people.

The colliery closed in 1952 due to a disastrous fire that started in the shaft. The site became the North West Area Training Centre for the National Coal Board and finally closed in 1989.

From *'THE REPORT OF THE INSPECTOR OF MINES'*.
23rd. September 1891.

At 2.30 am. in the 7th. hour of the shift Moss Heyes aged 66 years, a dataller, was repairing some brick arching close to the pit bottom when some bricks fell out above his head and killed him. He was accustomed to the work.

In Affectionate Memory of

SAMUEL COOK,
Aged 34 Years.

JAMES E. COOK,
Aged 36 Years.

THOMAS WOOLLAM,
Aged 47 Years.

DANIEL BAINES,
Aged 46 Years.

THOMAS WATERWORTH, Aged 42 Years,

Who were killed in the terrible disaster at the New Boston Pit, Haydock, on July 16, 1905.

Cut down so sudden ; oh, how sad !
We all do weep and mourn for thee ;
A lesson from this may be learned,
To prepare us all for eternity.

"In the midst of life we are in death."

Hand, L'pool.

REMEMBERANCE CARD FOR THE VICTIMS OF NEW BOSTON DISASTER OF 1905 (Mr. Bennet)

From **'THE REPORT OF THE INSPECTOR OF MINES'.**

29th. July 1900.

Mark Luke aged 51 years, a chargehand, Thomas Gillard aged 45 years, a sinker, James Hyens aged 33 years, Patrick Flaherty aged 35 years, Patrick King aged 26 years, James King aged 20 years, and Patrick Babe aged 40 years were killed when they were sinking No. 3 shaft to 245 yards.

They were loading dirt into the hoppet when the floor heaved up with an outburst of firedamp fired at one of the candles.

It was recommended that electric lights should be used.

OLD BOSTON COLLIERY (Mr. Simm)

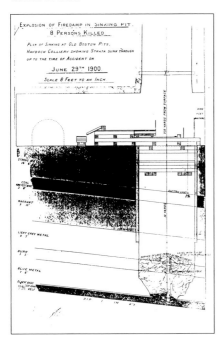

DIAGRAM OF THE DISASTER AT OLD BOSTON COLLIERY (Inspector's Report)

THE SCREENS AND HEADGEAR (Mr. Simm)

LADIES BATH AND CANTEEN (BC)

Wood pit was about a mile away from Boston colliery and did not have it's own pithead baths. Many people remember, with mixed feelings, the 'pit clog stampede' of pit black faces from Wood pit to the baths at Old Boston colliery at the end of the shift.

In the nineteen forties and fifties, women worked on the screens at the colliery.

Special provision was made for the ladies, by the National Coal Board.

The death of a man underground was an all too common occurrence but in good Lancashire tradition they were buried with due observance of the occasion. This is the bill for a colliers funeral. Mr. Ken Ashton was killed at Boston Colliery in February 1926.

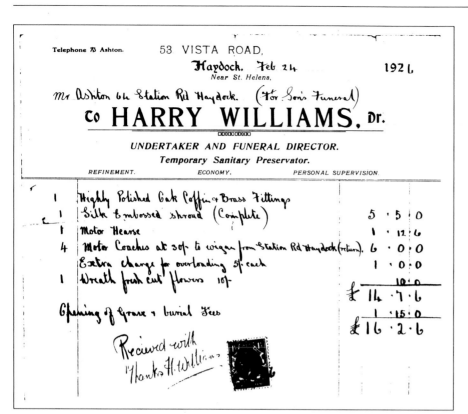

Telephone 70 Ashton.

53 VISTA ROAD,
Haydock. Feb 24   1926
Near St. Helens,

Mr Ashton 64 Station Rd Haydock. (For Son's Funeral)

co HARRY WILLIAMS, Dr.

UNDERTAKER AND FUNERAL DIRECTOR.
Temporary Sanitary Preservator.

REFINEMENT.   ECONOMY.   PERSONAL SUPERVISION.

1 Highly Polished Oak Coffin & Brass Fittings	
1 Silk Embossed shroud (Complete)	5 . 5 . 0
1 Motor Hearse	1 . 12 . 6
4 Motor Coaches at 30/- to wigan from Station Rd Haydock (return)	6 . 0 . 0
Extra charge for overloading 5/- each	1 . 0 . 0
1 Wreath fresh cut flowers 10/-	10 . 0
	£ 14 . 7 . 6
Opening of Grave & burial fees	1 . 15 . 0
	£ 16 . 2 . 6

Recieved with
Thanks H. Williams

MR. ASHTON'S FUNERAL BILL (Mr. K. Ashton)

OLD FOLD COLLIERY

This was situated east of West End Road, Haydock on Park Street. It was sunk by Richard Evans and Co. in the 1850's but it was not very profitable and closed fifteen years later.

OLD WHINT AND NEW WHINT COLLIERIES

Over the years, the spelling of the colliery and the area varies, from 'Whynt', 'Wynt' and as it is known today, 'Whint'. The colliery was situated at the end of Old Whint Road, Haydock. Several shafts were sunk but found to be unprofitable in the 1850's and they had very short lives.

PARKSIDE COLLIERY

NATIONAL COAL BOARD
(North Western Division)

✻

PROGRAMME

for the

Official Inauguration

of

THE NEW PARKSIDE COLLIERY

by

THE REV. JOHN H. BROADHURST
The Vicar of Newton-le-Willows

and

Mrs. G. G. H. BOLTON

✻

TUESDAY

28th MAY, 1957

at 11-15 a.m. for 11-45 a.m.

✻

Please reply on enclosed Post Card if you will be able to attend

SURFACE PLAN OF OLD BOSTON COLLIERY

THE OFFICIAL PROGRAMME OF THE OPENING OF PARKSIDE COLLIERY

THE HEADGEARS AT NIGHT (Mr. Simm)

Programme

11-15 a.m.

THE CLOCK FACE AND SUTTON MANOR COLLIERIES BAND will play.

11-45 a.m.

THE VICAR and MRS. G. G. H. BOLTON accompanied by COL. G. G. H. BOLTON (Divisional Chairman) and MR. J. ANDERTON (Area General Manager, No. 3 [St. Helens] Area) assemble on the dais and MR. ANDERTON will open the proceedings.

Then those present will accompany Mrs. Bolton from the dais and being arrived at the Foundation Stone, the following petition shall be voiced.

As we stand on the threshold of this great enterprise, we would remember before God those who have laboured to make our Country great by winning for us the wealth of the earth. Grant that the same spirit of adventure, of endurance, and of self sacrifice for the common weal may inspire those who engage in this undertaking, that it may be a noble tribute to our time.

Receiving the trowel, Mrs. Bolton shall then lay the Foundation Stone of Parkside Colliery.

DRAKE'S PRAYER

O Lord God, when Thou givest to Thy servants to endeavour any great matter, grant us also to know that it is not the beginning, but the continuing of the same until it be thoroughly finished, which yieldeth the true glory. Through Him that for the finishing of Thy work laid down His life—Thy Son Jesus Christ. Amen.

THE BLESSING

O God, bless this endeavour and all engaged in it. Those who hold positions of responsibility and have to make decisions ; the architects and planners, the builders, and the generations of those who will find employment here in the years to come. Give them wisdom in all they do, and shield them in the hazards of their calling, and may God be with them all, now and always. Amen.

The gathering will then sing the Hymn, during which the party will return to dais.

1

O God, our help in ages past,
　Our hope for years to come,
Our shelter from the stormy blast,
　And our eternal home.

2

Beneath the shadow of thy throne
　Thy saints have dwelt secure ;
Sufficient is thine arm alone,
　And our defence is sure.

3

Before the hills in order stood,
　Or earth received her frame,
From everlasting thou art God,
　To endless years the same.

4

A thousand ages in thy sight
　Are like an evening gone ;
Short as the watch that ends the night
　Before the rising sun.

5

Time, like an ever-rolling stream,
　Bears all its sons away ;
They fly forgotten, as a dream
　Dies at the opening day.

6

O god, our help in ages past,
　Our hope for years to come,
Be thou our guard while troubles last
　And our eternal home.

Miss Holme will present Mrs. Bolton with a Bouquet.

The Area General Manager will then invite Mrs. Bolton to speak.

GOD SAVE THE QUEEN

THE OFFICIAL PROGRAMME OF THE OPENING OF PARKSIDE COLLIERY (Mr. Simm)

Parkside colliery is the most recent colliery to start production in the area. It was built in the nineteen fifties and is one of the two surviving mines in production in 1990.

In November 1950 an exploratory borehole was sunk and between December 1951 and March 1957 a further twenty six boreholes were driven in the earth on the site.

A contract was given to Messers. Kinnear-Moodie for the shaft sinking and they worked in conjunction with a South African sinking contractor who provided sinking manager and a nucleus of skilled men.

Sinking started on 24th November 1957 on No. 1 shaft and on the 1st December on the No. 2 shaft. The final depth of the two shafts was approximately 890 yards.

The colliery was officially opened on 28th. May 1957.

THE PARR COLLIERIES

Parr Nos. 1 and 2 was known as the Havannah Colliery and Parr Nos. 4 and 5 as Southport Colliery. Both belonged to Richard Evans and Company. The records do not always show the colliery at which the incident took place.

From **'THE REPORT OF THE INSPECTOR OF MINES'.**
5th. August 1868.
James Potter aged 17 years, a drawer was drowned in the sump.

From **'THE REPORT OF THE INSPECTOR OF MINES'.**
PROSECUTIONS 1881.
Benjamin Wilkins was charged with firing a shot before examining the place for gas. He did not answer the charge as he had absconded.

Thomas Westwell was fined 10/- with costs for neglecting to set sprags.

Robert Duckworth was charged with having loose powder in the mine and was fined 15/- with costs.

A successful prosecution was sometimes displayed at the pit bank to remind others of the consequences.

HAVANNAH COLLIERY
(Parr Nos. 1 and 2.).

This was one of a group of collieries belonging to Messrs. Richard Evans and Company of Haydock. The Parr Collieries, part of the group comprised Southport Colliery (Parr Nos.4 and 5) and Havannah Colliery (Parr Nos.1 and 2). It was always known as 'The Vanny' in Haydock.

There was also a Parr No.3. It was situated close to Havannah Colliery and was used as a pumping pit.

Of the two collieries, Southport was the larger, employing over 700 men at it's peak. In the 1890's Havannah was reported as having a total of 580 men working two pits. The colliery closed in 1927, but was reopened in the 1930's to gain access to a small panel of coal. It was finally abandoned in 1936.

Havannah Colliery was well known for it's concrete enginehouse which stood for many years after the colliery closed.

From **'THE ST.HELENS LANTERN'.**
2nd. October 1891.
FAREWELL.
On Friday the workers said farewell to the late manager of the colliery Mr James Newton. Mr Arthur Span gave a short speech and presented Mr. Newton with a fine picture of Winwick church. There were further speeches and songs from some others.

A serious case of overwinding

occurred at the colliery on 6th. April 1875, when Edward Kay aged 25 years and John Francis aged 30 years both colliers were killed.

Mr. Henry Hall, the Mines Inspector, commented in his report for 1875 'A serious case of overwinding took place at the colliery. Various inventions have been brought before the public with a view to the prevention of this kind of accident but they all deal with the accident after it had happened. The most desirable arrangement would perhaps be some automatic gearing in connection with the winding engine to prevent the cage being wound beyond a certain point.

At the inquest into the deaths at the Primrose Vaults, Park Road, Parr was reported in the 'ST. HELENS STANDARD' on the 17th. April 1875.

John Francis the father of the deceased said that his son went to work at 5.30am and the first that he heard of the accident was at 4.30. p.m. when someone told him that his son had been 'pulled in'. This was not the first time that this had happened. Three weeks ago it had occurred and his son had told him that he had a horror of going to work.

Martha Kay said that her husband left home at 5 am. and was brought home in the afternoon complaining that his thigh was broken. She said he gave no account of the accident except the cage was going up very fast and he jumped out. He had complained about

HAVANNAH COLLIERY (Mr. Simm)

HAYDOCK, ASHTON, EDGE GREEN, PARR, AND GOLBORNE COLLIERIES.

On April 5th, 1889, at Parr Colliery, No. 2 Pit, in the Ravenhead Main Delf, Edward Briscoe, Collier, Unrammed a **ROBOURITE** SHOT in the presence of Richard Rigby, Fireman, and Peter Anders, Shotlighter. In consideration of the fact that Briscoe told what he had done, Messrs. Richd. Evans & Co. have **ONLY** dismissed him, and also Rigby and Anders.

NOTICE IS HEREBY GIVEN, that should any future case occur of this and all the parties concerned will be Prosecuted, as the Firm are determined to put a Stop to such **EXTREMELY**

DANGEROUS PRACTICES.

By Order,

RICHARD EVANS AND CO.

PROSECUTION NOTICE (Mr. Simm)

SCALE OF MINIMUM RATES FOR COLLIERS, DRAWERS, AND FILLERS.

AGE.	Basis Rate 1911	Minimum Rate 10%	15%	20%	23⅓%
14	2/3	2/6	2/7½	2/9	2/10
14½	2/6	2/9	2/10½	3/-	3/1
15	2/9	3/-	3/1½	3/3	3/4
15½	3/-	3/3	3/5	3/7	3/8
16	3/3	3/7½	3/9½	3/11½	4/1
16½	3/6	3/10½	4/0½	4/2½	4/4
17	3/9	4/1½	4/3½	4/5½	4/7
17½	4/-	4/4½	4/7	4/9½	4/11
18	4/4	4/10	5/0½	5/3	5/4½
18½	4/8	5/2	5/5	5/8	5/10
19	5/-	5/6	5/9	6/-	6/2
19½	5/3	5/9	6/-	6/3	6/5
20 and over	5/6	6/-	6/3½	6/7	6/9

Agreement as to Sharers and Drawers.

Each workman to whom the Act applies, at present employed by the Company, to at once definitely state whether he is working as Collier, Drawer, or Sharer, and a record of this shall be entered in the Company's books, and shall in future be taken as final evidence as to the classification of employment.

When a workman is first signed on he shall state whether he intends working as a Collier, Drawer, or Sharer.

Before any alteration shall be *bona-fide* the employee shall notify the Management of the Company by giving one week's notice of any change. Until such notice is given the original classification shall hold good.

COLLIERS' DAYWAGE COALING AND MINIMUM RATES.

	Basis Rate 1911	Minimum Rate 10%	15%	20%	23⅓%
Collier when getting Coal by Day wage or in abnormal place	7/6	8/3	8/7½	9/-	9/3
Drawer ,, ,, ,,	6/-	6/7¼	6/10¾	7/2½	7/4¾
Collier Datalling	5/8	6/3	6/6½	6/10	7/-
Drawing Datalling	5/3	5/9	6/-	6/3	6/5
Colliers' Minimum Rate	6/6	7/1½	7/5½	7/9½	8/-
For Adult Drawer sharing with Collier	6/-	6/7½	6/11	7/2½	7/5
Drawer over 20 years and under 21 sharing with Collier	5/9	6/4½	6/8	6/11½	7/2

The Minimum Rate is payable weekly, provided men have worked 80 per cent. of the time the Pit has worked, unless prevented by illness or accident, or other justifiable cause.

Where three men are working together and sharing the joint earnings, two should rank as Colliers and one as Drawer.

The following persons are also entitled to the Colliers' Minimum Rate if they work by piece and fail to earn the Minimum Rate :—

(*a*) The man in charge of the place whilst Coal-cutting is being done by a Long-wall Face Machine.

(*b*) The men responsible for the getting down and heaking out of the coal after the machine, and timbering of the place when the coal is broken out.

Explosives free when men are in Abnormal or Minimum Wage places.

COLLIERS AND DRAWERS WAGES 1916 (Mr. McGuirk)

the engineer before now.

Henry Lowe the Certificated Manager at the colliery who resided on the premises, said he had been informed of the accident by a pit brow girl and went to the No 2 downcast shaft to find that the cage was entangled with the headgear.

The two injured men were transported home in a cart with plenty of straw and they were obviously badly hurt. Someone said that another had fallen down the shaft. A new cage was rigged and sent down for the men at work. Sixty men were brought out and the last was the body of Francis.

David Mercer the browman was at his post and Thomas Atherton the hooker-on said that the signals were given as usual and the cage went up. He saw the empty cage come down faster than usual and heard a noise and found it broken at the bottom. He afterwards found the body of Francis at the pit bottom.

Sarah Bradley worked on the pit brow to put in the catches said as the cage came up it went past her and she put her hands over her eyes. Henry Potter (Sen). said that the method of working the indicator was an old one and Henry Potter (Jnr.), the engineman, said that a piece of iron came through the roof and struck his arm. He said that he saw that the cage had gone too far and reversed the engine. The engine itself was an old locomotive, 'The Sultan' and the pit was 340 yards deep. Mr Hall the inspector said that the indicator was not satisfactory.

Edward Smith said that eleven weeks ago the cage containing John Daniel, James Pye, James Critchley and the deceased, Francis, was taken up and not down.

The jury took twenty minutes and found that the engineman was guilty of negligence and that the management were guilty of not maintaining the indicator. A charge of manslaughter was preferred against the engineman and he was released on bail of £50 and committed to the next assizes.

PARR No. 1 PIT.—PRICE LIST.

MINE	Basis Rate 1911	Minimum Rate 10%	15%	20%	23⅓%
HIGHER FLORIDA :—					
Strait and Pillar, per ton	1/9¾	2/-	2/1	2/2	2/2¾
Widework, End or Face ,,	2/1½	2/4	2/5¼	2/6½	2/7½
Yards on Face	5/9	6/4	6/7½	6/10¾	7/1
Yards on End	6/3	6/10½	7/2¼	7/6	7/8½
Yards, Ribbing................	2/11	3/2½	3/4¼	3/6	3/7¼
LOWER FLORIDA :—					
Strait and Pillar, per ton ..	1/7¼	1/9¼	1/10¼	1/11¼	1/11¾
Widework, End on face, ,,	1/10½	2/0¾	2/2	2/3¼	2/4
Yards on face................	5/9	6/4	6/7½	6/10¾	7/1
Yards on End	6/3	6/10½	7/2¼	7/6	7/8½
Yards on Ribbing	2/11	3/2½	3/4¼	3/6	3/7¼
YARD COAL :—					
Widework, per ton	2/2½	2/5	2/6½	2/7¾	2/8¾

Prices subject to percentages as from December 1st, 1915, *i.e.*, from Minimum Rate shown in list.

WAGES FOR THE PARR NO. 1 PIT (Mr. McGuirk)

From ***'THE REPORT OF THE MINES INSPECTOR'.***
2nd. December 1887.

Joseph Hancock aged 24 years, a shunter was killed when some waggons were being shunted into the colliery from the main line. He was putting down the brake when the waggon he was on, was pushed forward and he was crushed.

From ***'THE REPORT OF THE MINES INSPECTOR'.***
25th. June 1923.

Robert Heyes aged 60 years, a dataller, was killed at 8.45 am. in the first hour of the shift. He was walking down an empty road where it passed a haulage crossover. Two tubs were coming down and he did not hear them as he was a little deaf.

A copy of the wage structure at the colliery for 1916 has survived.

The Parr No.2 pit worked the Ravenhead Higher and Main Delf seams and the Nine Feet Seam. The No.4 pit worked the Rushy Park and Little Delf Seams and the No.5 pit the Nine Feet Seam.

A table of colliers and drawers wages also survives for 1916.

SOUTHPORT COLLIERY

(Parr 4 & 5).

The colliery was situated between Newton Road and the canal-end of Southport Street. This colliery was one of the Parr Collieries belonging to Richard Evans & Co. Ltd. It was sunk in 1892, soon after the firm had been made into a limited company. The 'Inspector's Report' for 1894, records the colliery just starting up, with only 200 men working there. The colliery was expanded greatly in the present century, employing in the region of 1,000 men. It was finally abandoned in 1936, when it flooded and over 500 men lost their jobs.

SOUTHPORT COLLIERY (Dr. Holden)

From 'THE REPORT OF THE MINES INSPECTOR'.

12th. September 1892.

The shaft had just been completed and several men were engaged in opening out the roadways when the explosion took place. The certificated manager went down and he and two others were overcome by fumes and died. Those who died were Thomas Sharrock aged 41 years, the manager of the colliery, Peter Cook aged 24 years, a fireman, and Thomas Ball aged 28 years, a collier.

PARR DAM AND PARR MILL COLLIERIES

These collieries were situated near Parr Greyhound Stadium. Both these collieries operated in the 1820's and 1830's. Parr Dam colliery was owned by Nicholas Ashton and later worked by Charles Orrell from the nearby Parr Mill colliery. Records show they were closed in 1840.

PARR STOCKS COLLIERY

The colliery was situated at the St. Helens end of Fleet Lane. This colliery first appeared in the records in 1832, when a Joseph Greenough was working it. The 'Inspector's Reports' for 1850 and 1855 show the colliery being owned by Johnson, Weninck and Co. A report in the 'St. Helens Intelligencer' of the 1st May, 1858, states that the colliery was for sale.

PEASLEY CROSS COLLIERY

In 1855 the colliery was known as Peasley House Colliery and was owned by Bournes Robinson.

From 'THE COLLIERY GUARDIAN'.

1st. March 1858.

On Tuesday last, at the new colliery owned by Bournes Robinson and Company, Aaron Wedgewood and George Twist were engaged in sinking.

They had prepared two shots for blasting and, having lit the fuses, they ascended the shaft when one of the charges exploded but not the other.

They descended and found the second shot covered with stones and debris. When they were examining it, it exploded throwing stones in all directions. One hit Wedgewood in the forehead inflicting a sever fracture of the temporal bone. He died shortly after and Twist escaped with a few slight bruises.

From 'THE ST.HELENS NEWSPAPER'
14th. January 1865.

Thomas Gardiner who was a police constable until November and stationed at Peasley Cross was now working as a labourer removing waggons from under the riddle. He was found crushed between waggons. He was 28 years old and lived in Ormskirk Street.

From 'THE COLLIERY GUARDIAN'.
20th. October 1871.
ACCIDENT AT THE PEASLEY CROSS.

James Burrows, a collier aged 41 years, was suffocated by chokedamp when he was sent into a working to see if there was gas in a cavity. When he did not return, his father went in after him. He was found dead and removed with difficulty due to the gas which was thought to have come from the town's sewers.

In 1879 the Certificated Manager was William Lee who was also the manager at the Sherdley Colliery and it was recorded that there were no deaths at the colliery.

In 1882 Mr.Robert Turner was the Certificated Manager and also managed the Sherdley Colliery for the company.

By 1894, the colliery was owned by the Whitecross Company Limited, of Warrington and the manager was Mr.Robert Turner whose Certificate number was 709. The undermanagers were Mr.R. Armstrong (Certificate No.2436, 2nd class), Mr.J, French (Certificate No.1312, 2nd class) and Mr. J.Harrison (Certificate No.1313, 2nd class). The colliery employed 185 men and boys underground and 80 people on the surface.

COAL DECLARATION.
PEASLEY-CROSS COLLIERY.

COAL DECLARATION 1861 (Mr. Atherton)

PEWFALL COLLIERY

The colliery was situated on the north side of Liverpool Road, Ashton-in-Makerfield and was sunk by Samuel Clough. Richard Evans and Co. bought the colliery from the executors of Samuel after his death. The 'Inspector's Report' of 1894 reported that the colliery employed 220 people and had four shafts.

By the end of the century only two shafts were working. At it's peak production the colliery raised 130,000 tons of coal per year. The colliery closed in 1911.

From 'THE WIGAN EXAMINER'.
29th. March 1854.

The inquest into the death of Thomas Ashurst, collier at Samuel Clough's colliery in Pewfall, was held in the house of Joseph Radcliffe. Some coal fell on him and killed him on the 20th. The verdict was 'accidental death'.

Mr. Clough wrote a letter to the court saying that he thought highly of Ashurst. He gave £3 to the widow and the children and provided an oak coffin.

From 'THE WIGAN OBSERVER'.
24th. April 1857.

On Saturday last, at the colliery owned by Mr. Samuel Clough and under the management of Mr. Frost, Mr. Frost was at the pit mouth on the lower stage, looking over the barrier with the cage above him.

While he was standing like this, the cage was accidentally set in motion and struck him on the head. The whole of the lower jaw and part of the face were torn away and he fell down the shaft.

The mangled body was recovered and he was attended to by a doctor but he died on Sunday. He left a wife and two children.

A fragment of his gravestone survives in St. Thomas's church yard Ashton. It is rare for someone killed at a colliery to have the event recorded on a stone.

From 'THE COLLIERY GUARDIAN'.
21st. November 1868.
FIRE AT THE COLLIERY.

The fire broke out about 1 pm. on Thursday in a hut at the pit brow. When it was discovered people carried buckets of water one hundred yards to try to bring it under control and Mr. J. Evans was soon on the scene. He took over but after about an hour it became evident that they were fighting a loosing battle.

Mr. Bell, the Superintendent of the St. Helens Fire Brigade was sent for and arrived half an hour later. By this time the fire had spread from the hut to the headgear, a platform and almost everything else at the pit brow. It had started to encroach on the new engine house and about two to three hundred tons of slack caught fire.

At this point it seemed a hopeless task but it was finally brought under control after nine hours. It was estimated that about £2,500 of damage had been done and the colliery was not insured against such loss.

From 'THE COLLIERY GUARDIAN'.
January 1869.

It is reported that water has broken into the colliery in consequence of the excavations for the Lancashire Union Railway and three hundred men are out of employment.

Some of the men went to work at the Queen pit and were killed in the explosion at that colliery in June.

From 'THE REPORT OF THE MINES INSPECTOR'.
6th. January 1863.

Roger Dowd aged 31 years who worked as a jigger was killed when he was drawn by the chain against the drum.

From 'THE ST.HELENS STANDARD'.
3rd. March 1866.
FATAL ACCIDENT.

At the inquest at the Owl's Nest Inn, Blackbrook on Timothy Winstanley, a collier residing at Prescott's Entry, Blackbrook, Mr William Pickard, the Miners Agent was present.

The first witness was Joseph Strong the fireman at the colliery. He said that the deceased was fifty three years old and on Wednesday last at about 11 am. he was drilling a hole at the bottom of the coal for a shot.

A prop taker had been working in the place and there were two rows of props on the lower side and three on the higher. The fireman was satisfied with the place and everything was made safe. He left the place after his inspection and after about a quarter of an hour heard someone call out.

On investigation he found that a portion of the roof had fallen knocking out two or three of Winstanley's props and driving them over into his working place. One of them had come to rest against his shoulder and was pressing his face against the wall. With some assistance he managed to release him and he said 'Joseph, get me out of this place'. He never spoke again.

He was got out of the pit and taken home an a cart. There did not seem that there was very much wrong with him except the side of his head which was severely injured. He was an old and experienced collier but not over careful.

James Ashton was called who was working two places away and took him home. He said that Dr. Twyford was called

MR. FROST'S GRAVESTONE

COLLIERS AT THE PIT HEAD (SMM)

for but Dr. Jameson came and he never moved after that.

William Sanders was his drawer and was at the place when the accident happened. Verdict 'accidental death'.

From 'THE ST.HELENS NEWSPAPER AND ADVERTISER'.

5th. January 1867.

COLLIERY ACCIDENT AT PEWFALL COLLIERY.

The works at this colliery are very extensive and there are three shafts in the area of an acre.

An explosion took place at No. 4 Little Delf Mine 400 yards in depth, and resulted in the injuring of two men seriously, Patrick Maloney and John Clarke, so much that it was some days before they were out of danger, In fact on Friday evening it was rumoured that Clarke was dead.

Joseph Williams, William Smethurst, William Brown and another who was not named were also among the injured. Work was resumed at the colliery on Friday.

COLLIERS DRINKING (SMM)

From *'THE REPORT OF THE INSPECTOR OF MINES'*.
16th. June 1874.

James Burnside aged 40 years, a furnaceman in the No.4 pit was suffocated by No 3 pit taking fire. Both pits were sealed. The body was recovered in December.

At the pit, steps are being taken to find out if there is any one down the pit at the time of the fire. The pit was closed at the time for the Newton races and only the furnace tenter was down.

Ash from the furnace is believed to be the cause of the fire and the pit became full of smoke and the tenter was suffocated.

From *'THE REPORT OF THE INSPECTOR OF MINES'*.
8th. April 1884.

Henry Horne aged 21 years, a dataller, was working for a contractor in the No. 3 pit who let him take a tub down a brow of seven inches to the yard with only a drill as a scotch.

The tub overpowered him and he was flung against a prop breaking his skull.

The contractor was very negligent of his duty and the man had only recently come into the pit and knew little of it's dangers.

The photographs are believed to be colliers at the colliery and a group of Pewfall colliers relaxing round the table, supping ale, a pastime that has survived to the present day.

From *'THE COLLIERY GUARDIAN'*.
30th. January 1885.

Edward Conroy, the fireman was charged with neglecting the furnace and leaving before the night man came.

John Simon, the engineman, was charged with not preventing him leaving and George Strong was charged with being down the pit when he was not employed there.. It was stated that they wanted to go to a football match and Simon said that he left the furnace at 5.30 pm, ten minutes early. He was fined 40/- plus costs.

From *'THE REPORT OF THE INSPECTOR OF MINES'*.
4th. June 1885.

There was an explosion of gas at the No. 3 colliery in the Little Delf Mine when the barometer read 29.91 ins and was falling.

A shotlighter was going to fire a shot and on examining the place found a little gas on the higher side which had accumulated in consequence of his neglect to set up a brattice cloth. He brushed it out with one of the colliers shirts and then proceeded to light the fuse when a small quantity of gas exploded.

The injuries that the man received were so slight that he did not leave work. The shotlighter was charged with a breach of the Rules for not withdrawing his men from a dangerous part of the mine and fined 40/- with costs.

From *'THE REPORT OF THE INSPECTOR OF MINES'*.
7th. JULY 1888.

Henry Burrows aged 40 years, a fireman, and James Dearden aged 36 years, a dataller, were killed when they were retimbering an old road in the No. 3 pit which was crushed. After setting a bar, they were taking out the old one when the side came over carrying two bars with it.

From *'THE ST.HELENS LANTERN'*.
6th. November 1891.

John Smethurst, an unmarried man of Lower Lane, Pewfall, was engaged in the colliery when a portion of the roof fell on his back and badly crushed him. He was taken home and lies in a precarious state.

PHOENIX COLLIERY

The colliery was situated on Burtonhead Road. This colliery was opened by Benjamin B. Glover in 1873, when the 'Inspector's Report' showed that one pit was in the process of being sunk. The 'Colliery Guardian' for 1893, records two pits 85 and 90 yards in depth, with an advanced arrangement of winding, ventilating and haulage machinery. The output

---

PEWFALL PIT.
RUSHY PARK MINE.

Wide work, no yards, no bars... | 1/2 |

PRICES NOT SUBJECT TO PERCENTAGES.

Payment for parting dirt between tops and bottoms over 9 in. thick, 1 d. per ton extra, with an additional 1d. per ton for every 4 in.

For opening out wide work places when fallen up across whole width to pay one day's wage (*i.e.* 5s. plus current per centage) for cutting in 3 yards wide (with liberty to widen out to 4 yards), and 2d. per ton extra. If fallen on one side, 1d. per ton extra.

Wide work : On end of coal, 2d. per ton extra.

LITTLE DELPH MINE.

Wide work, no yards, no bars... | 1/5 |

PRICES NOT SUBJECT TO PERCENTAGES.

For opening out wide work places when fallen up across whole width to pay one day's wage (*i.e.* 5s. plus current per centage) for cutting in 3 yards wide (with liberty to widen out to 4 yards), and 2d. per ton extra. If fallen on one side, 1d. per ton extra.

Holeing and removing flooring dirt up to 9in. in thickness, 1d. per ton extra.

Wide work : On end of coal, 2d. per ton extra.

Colliers working in making out places	5/-
Drawers working in making out places	4/-
Men to find explosives.	
Colliers' day wage	3/10
Drawers	3/6

PRICES NOT SUBJECT TO PERCENTAGES.

Crabbing, or pushing up on the dip of the mine after the first 13 yards, 1d. per ton down to 26 yards, and an additional 1d. per ton for every 10 yards afterwards.

Long Drawing.—Where drawing exceeds 150 yards on level, 1d. per ton extra up to 200 yards, and 1d. per ton for every additional 50 yards.

Where drawing exceeds 100 yards up brow, 1d. per ton extra, and 1d. per ton for every additional 50 yards over 100 yards.

Filling tanks with water, 3d. per small tank and 6d. per large tank.

Filling and emptying boxes with dirt, 8d. per box including drawing, if beyond drawing limit 1d. per box extra - 4d. per box if filled only ; emptied only, 4d. per box,

Setting 7 ft. bars, 5d. per bar.

Setting prop chocks, 4 ft. 6 in. square, filled with dirt, 9d. each ; and prop chocks above 4 ft. 6 in. high to be paid in like proportion.

Drawing props, 1d. per prop.

PRICES AT THE HAYDOCK COLLIERIES FOR COAL GETTING AS IN 1888, AT PEWFALL PIT.

THE LANCASHIRE COALFIELD.
XXI.—Phœnix Colliery.

The colliery is situated about one mile west of St. Helens station on the London and North-Western Railway, and ten miles east-north-east of Liverpool, the lessees being Messrs. Glover, Urmson and Glover, of St. Helens. Two shafts are sunk at the plant now in operation, about 60 yards apart in a north and south line. The winding and downcast shaft is 10 ft. in diameter and 90 yards in depth to the Lower Pigeon House seam. The upcast shaft is placed north of the winding shaft, also 10 ft. in diameter and 85 yards in depth to the same seam. It is used principally as the ventilating or upcast shaft for the mine. The main hauling engine is placed near the top, and the hauling rope passes through the shaft to work the downbrow in the Lower Pigeon House Mine. An air-compressor is placed on the surface near the downcast shaft to work several pumps placed in different parts of the downbrow underground, also to actuate haulage engines in course of erection at the bottom of the downbrow. The ventilation of the mine is produced by a Guibal fan, placed near the top of the upcast shaft, driven by duplicate engines alternately. The coal produced is consumed largely in St. Helens for house and manufacturing purposes, and is also used extensively as a steam coal.

Winding.—The winding and hauling engines are placed between and in line with the two shafts. The winding engine at the downcast has two horizontal cylinders 16 in. by 30 in., ordinary slide-valves, plain drum 4½ ft. in diameter, brake ring or fly-wheel 8½ ft. in diameter, acted upon by a strap above and another on the underside of the wheel, both straps being lined with flat hemp rope. One tub of 6 cwt. capacity is raised in each cage, there being two wire rope conductors to a cage. A small engine with vertical cylinder, 9 in. by 30 in., is placed near the top of the upcast shaft, and is provided chiefly for raising men and materials in case of a breakdown at the other winding engine. The winding ropes in each case are of plough steel, and each rope is fitted with an Ormerod detaching hook.

Air Compressor.—There is one steam cylinder 15 in. diameter, 3½ ft. stroke, and one air cylinder of the same dimensions, with fly-wheel, all in line. The normal air-pressure is 40 lb. in the two receivers, the air is carried through the downcast and to the bottom of the south downbrow (which has an inclination of 1 in 4) in 4 in. pipes, the full dip of the measures being 1 in 3½, varying from south to south-east. There are three pumps at the bottom of the downbrow, each of which has an air motor, 8 in. by 8 in., working a single ram pump of 4 in. diameter. At the rate of 40 strokes per minute, these pumps will force 39 gals. of water to a cistern 350 yards higher up the brow, where two horizontal pumps are placed, the air-motors being each 14 in. by 12 in. stroke, driving two 5 in. rams, which force 62 gals. of water (calculated at the same speed) to the bottom of the shaft, a distance of 550 yards. The air pipes are 4 in. in diameter, and the water pipes 3 in. diameter. There are two larger pumps at the bottom of the downcast shaft to force the water to the surface; these consist of two air motors, 14 in. by 12 in. stroke, driving two 6 in. rams. At the above speed the pumps will deliver 89 gals. per minute to the surface through 4 in. mains. The air-compressor and the motors and pumps referred to were constructed by Messrs. J. Slee and Co., of Earlestown; the compressor being fitted with air-valves patented by Messrs. Pilkington and Forrest.

Underground Hauling.—The hauling engine on the surface before named has two horizontal cylinders, 15 in. by 30 in., geared 1 to 4, and one drum 6 ft. in diameter. The hauling rope is of plough steel, ¾ in. diameter, which passes through wooden boxes in the upcast shaft. Sets of eighteen to twenty tubs of 6 cwt. capacity are hauled up the downbrow, and the empties run down with the rope, the gradient being 1 in 4. The following is a sketch of the south downbrow, showing the position of the shafts, underground pumps, and hauling engines.

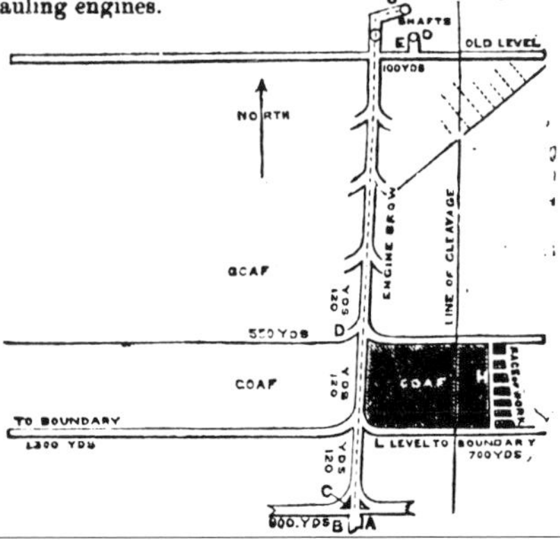

D is the downcast shaft, U the upcast shaft, the hauling rope running up and down the same. At A is placed the hauling air engine for the east level, another at B for the west level; these engines will do away with the employment of horses entirely. At C are placed the three pumps worked by compressed air forcing water up to D. The two pumps at D force water to the bottom of the shaft at E. At the point E two horizontal pumps are placed which force water to the surface, the motive power both for D and E pumps being compressed air.

Method of Working.—This is also shown on the sketch, the crossgate, H, being formed from the level, L, uphill, to the level 120 yards higher up; as it is being made the gateways are turned off to the east 12 yards apart from the centres, and the whole of the space between (10 yards in breadth) is packed up with stone obtained from ripping the top in the gateways. The level, L, is made 8 ft. wide and 7 ft. high, as are also the crossgates. The gateways are made 6 ft. wide and 4 ft. 6 in. high; the latter will be cut off by a new gateway 80 yards further east. The face of the coal is worked against the cleavage. Firedamp is rarely found in the workings, but safety lamps are used exclusively away from the shaft. The explosives used are tonite on the east side of the mine and compressed powder on the west side, these being used for ripping top only. It is stated that with tonite no flame is given out if the saw-dust compound furnished by the makers is placed in the shot-hole in front of the cartridge. The shots are fired with fuse by a shot-lighter, from 4 to 6 p.m. The Lower Pigeon House seam is only 2 ft. in thickness, so that the waste is barely sufficient to hold the *débris* resulting from ripping top in the gateways. In point of safety this filling up of the waste is desirable wherever it can be put in practice; the roof settles down and compresses it so that no space for the lodgment of gas can occur.

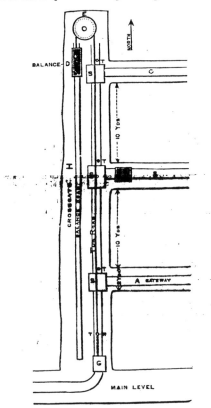

MAIN LEVEL

The second sketch is a plan of the apparatus for raising and lowering the tubs in the upbrow or crossgate, H, shown on first sketch. By the arrangement shown, the whole of the work from nine or ten stalls is sent down the brow on a declivity of 1 in 4, by means of a balance wagon, D (running on rails 14 in. gauge), a sheave, E, and ⅜ in. steel rope. Only three gateways are shown to exemplify the principle. The weight of the balance wagon is about intermediate between the weight of a laden and empty tub; it regulates the speed of the descending tub, and afterwards raises the empty tub to any gateway required. A plate, S, is required at the end of each gateway, on which the tubs are turned, and a spike, t, fixed in a sleeper for attaching the chain, which is 7 ft. long. The empty tub is now shown to be at G, and the balance at the top; suppose this tub is required to go into gateway B, the link at R is released from the spike, t, and the balance wagon at once descends and raises the tub to B, regulated by the attendant, the upper link R of the chain is then attached to the spike, t, holds the rope in position while the attendant attaches the back end of the chain to the tub, L, which is standing ready. This tub is then brought upon the iron plate, and turned into position to descend to the main level, the attendant pulling up the balance wagon at the same time to the top. The same explanation applies to any other gateway where a tub is required.

Ventilation.—The ventilation of the mine is produced by a fan of the Guibal type, constructed by Messrs. Walker Brothers, of Wigan, and erected in 1880. It is 18 ft. in diameter, 7 ft. in width, driven direct by an engine 12 in. by 24 in., and a duplicate alternately, the engine and fan running at present at a speed of 100 revolutions per minute.

Surface Hauling.—There is a small hauling engine on the surface, which hauls the railway wagons a distance of about 200 yards between the pit and sidings, by means of main and tail ropes of plough steel. The engine has two horizontal cylinders, 8 in. by 16 in., geared 1 to 4, two drums 2 ft. diameter, and hauls sets of six wagons each way. It was constructed by John Varley and Co., St. Helens.

Boilers.—There are three Lancashire boilers, one of which is of the Galloway type. Two boilers are 30 ft. by 8 ft., and one 28 ft. by 7 ft. An old boiler is utilised for heating feed-water by exhaust steam from the compressor to about 120 degs. temperature. The working pressure of steam is 45 lb.

The output of coal at this colliery is about 300 tons per day. The arrangements generally are of the most approved kind; the ventilating fan has more than once warded off accidents. No furnaces or boilers are found in this mine, and the heavy consumption of coal that furnaces entail is saved. The main downbrow haulage is performed by steam power on the surface transmitted by rope to the underground work, and compressed-air motors will be brought into service to act as feeders to the main line, horse labour being dispensed with entirely. It is difficult to account for the persistency with which furnaces are retained in mines for purposes of ventilation in Lancashire, considering the disadvantages and danger appertaining to their use. The alternative method of ventilating by means of fans of various types, offer so many inducements to their adoption, in point of safety, economy and efficiency, that it is not too much to say that, in another decade, the use of the furnace will be a thing of the past.

M. E.

Account of Patent Fuel Exported during the month of December 1892.*

FROM CARDIFF (including Penarth)

	Tons.
Bayonne	187
Brest	130
Bordeaux	205
Boucau	257
Iquique	2,693
La Guayra	500
Marseilles	400
Molfetta	200
Palma	460
Puerto Cabello	630
Rio Grande do Sul	400
Trinidad	3,142
Vera Cruz	4,315
Valencia	700
Venice	1,520
	15,739

FROM NEWPORT, MON.

	Tons.
Algiers	2,142
Buenos Ayres	1,410
Oran	947
	4 499

FROM SWANSEA.
(Including Neath, Port Talbot and Port Cawl.)

	Tons.
Algiers	2,245
Arzew	1,085
Bordeaux	2,560
Bona	1,162
Cherbourg	212
Charente	1,053
Dieppe	773
Civita Vecchia	1,536
Havre	165
Leghorn	1,249
L'Orient	148
Nantes	95
Naples	1,301
Phillippeville	621
Palermo	1,300
St. Nazaire	4,253
St. Malo	788
Torre Annunziata	1,350
Venice	2,900
	24,796

was given as 300 tons per day from the Lower Pigeon House Seam, which was only 2 ft. thick. The colliery employed 211 men. The colliery reputedly closed in 1895.

From *'THE REPORT OF THE MINES INSPECTOR'.*
16th. February 1882.

There was an explosion of gas in the Pigeon House seam at the colliery when one man was killed. The barometer read 30.32 ins. and was rising.

A little gas had collected during the night on the higher side of some widework face which the fireman did not discover in the morning and accordingly reported it safe.

The collier went in with an open candle in his hand and worked for an hour before the gas exploded.

Cause 'open lights'. In future the mine will be worked only with lamps.

From *'THE REPORT OF THE MINES INSPECTOR.*
22nd. November 1886.

At St. Helens Court the following of the colliery were all charged with having a pipe down the mine and fined 7/6d. plus costs. William Greenall, William Wilderman,

George Bibby, Thomas Bramlow, William Henshall, Richard Pye and Joseph Cubbins.

Patrick Tierney was fined 2/6d. plus costs for the same offence. Peter Roosey was fined 2/6d. and costs for having matches in the mine.

POCKET NOOK COLLIERY

From *'THE COLLIERY GUARDIAN'.*
July 1858.

There was an accident at the colliery belonging to Mr. R. Walker which caused the death of William Whittle the hooker-on.

The inquest was at the Queens Arms at Parr on Thursday and Mr. Higson the Government Inspector heard that a large quantity of stones fell from the side of the shaft onto him. Verdict, 'accidental death'.

From *'THE ST.HELENS NEWSPAPER'.*
4th. January 1862.

On Tuesday morning Joseph Ashton, the fireman in the Potato Delf Mine was in the mine when one of the rails on the waggon way got displaced.

The deceased was at work with a man named Michael Cullin when they were repairing the tramway which was nine feet

across. *The roof was not supported by any timber and he knelt down to nail the rail and three cwt. of rock and earth fell on him crushing his head.*

Cullin called for assistance which arrived in a few minutes. He was released alive and taken home where he died at midnight.

The inquest was at the Fleece Hotel. It was thought that the management was not satisfactory and they had been negligent in not supporting the roof. The deceased was aged 23 years and lived in Duke Street.

PRINCESS COLLIERY

This was one of the Haydock Collieries owned by Richard Evans and Co. It was situated close to King, Queen and Legh pits.

From *'THE WIGAN OBSERVER.'*
14th. June 1890.
OPENING OF NEW COLLIERY IN HAYDOCK.

On Tuesday afternoon, Miss. McDonald, sister-in-law of Mr T.D. Grimke, cut the first sod of a new pit which Messrs. Evans and Co. are opening. The pit will be known as

PRINCESS COLLIERY

the 'Princess' and is situate between Queen and Legh pits.

Amongst the spectators were Mr. T. D. Grimke, Managing Director, Mr. John Robinson, Chief Mining Engineer, Mr. R. Bradshaw, Accountant, Mr. E. Bielby, Estate Agent, Mr. E. J. George, Secretary, Mr. E. Jackson, Cashier, Mr. John Latham, Mr. James Forrest and other officials.

The shaft is to be sunk by Mr. Stevenson, contractor of Wigan.

From 'THE WIGAN OBSERVER'.
24th December 1892.
COLLIERY DEVELOPMENTS AT HAYDOCK.
The Princess Pit Haydock.

One of the pits included in Messrs. Evans and Co. Ltd. Sinking operations, which has been going on for some years has now been completely 'caged' and is now winding coal.

The pit is a new one and it has been sunk to a depth of 360 yards. Two very valuable seams of coal have been struck, known as the Rushy Park or Arley, and the Little Delph or Orrell, and a very considerable output is expected shortly.

The cages are two deck and will raise six boxes at once. The pit had been connected with King Pit, which has been sunk to two hundred yards deeper for the purpose. The King Pit is at present winding coal but will eventually be used as an upcast or air shaft for the Princess Pit.

From 'THE NEWTON AND EARLESTOWN GUARDIAN'.
7th. January 1898.
A HAYDOCK MINER CRUSHED TO DEATH.

On Monday evening Mr. Brighouse, the County Coroner, held an inquest of the death of Joseph Molyneaux, a collier living at Lime Kiln Lane, Haydock, who met with fatal injuries at Princess Pit, Haydock on Wednesday last and died on Friday morning.

Mr. Matthews Inspector, of Mines and, Mr. Watkinson, the Certificated Manager of the colliery, were present along with other gentlemen.

Ann Molyneaux of the same address said that the deceased was her husband and he was 35 years of age. She last saw him on Wednesday morning when he went to work and she was at the hospital when he died on Friday.

Frederick Speakman gave evidence that he was his drawer and was working with the deceased. They had commenced work at about eight and the fireman, Coyle, came to visit them before breakfast and one or two props had been set on the side of the place at the firemans visit.

When the fall came there was no room for any more props. The deceased seemed to think it was quite safe and if he had wanted more timber there was plenty there. The deceased asked him to fill the last few shovels of coal. They got down to the bottom coal and were going to get earth down when the deceased knocked out one prop and struck at the second and the roof came down on top of him. Mr. Speakman said he did not see any breaks on the roof.

Coyle, the fireman, stated that he had visited the deceased, who was a good collier. He did not see any slips before the accident but he did see one afterwards.

Mr. Watkinson, the manager of the pit, said that Coyle had been a fireman for 18 months and that he was a very capable man.

The jury returned a verdict of accidental death.

From 'THE REPORT OF THE MINES INSPECTOR'.
24th. September 1898.

John F. Parry aged 24 years, a dataller, was sitting down waiting for a hammer, when a stone fell from the side of the roadway injuring him slightly in the back. He died from inflammation of the brain in Haydock Cottage Hospital 1st February 1899.

From 'THE REPORT OF THE MINES INSPECTOR'.
18th. June 1898.

Elizabeth Rowley a waggon setter of

PRINCESS PIT.
RUSHY PARK MINE.

Stret work.

4 yds. wide on face, no tonnage	7/2
4 yds. wide on end	7/10
Wide work, no yards, no bars	1/2

PRICES NOT SUBJECT TO PERCENTAGES.

Payment for parting dirt between tops and bottoms over 9 in. thick, 1d. per ton extra, with an additional 1d. per ton for every 4 in.

For opening out wide work places, when fallen up across whole width, to pay one day's wage (i.e., 5s. plus current per centage) for cutting in 3 yds. wide (with liberty to widen out to 4 yds.), and 2d. per ton extra. If fallen on one side, 1d. per ton extra.

In Stret work: Setting 12 ft. bars 1s., setting 7 ft. bars 5d.

Wide work: On end of coal, 2d. per ton extra.

LITTLE DELF MINE.

Stret work.

4 yds. wide, no tonnage, on face	6/5 per yd.
4 yds. wide, no tonnage, on end	7/1 per yd.
Wide work, no yards, no bars	1/5

PRICES NOT SUBJECT TO PERCENTAGES.

For opening out wide work places, when fallen up across whole width, to pay one day's wage (i.e., 5s. plus current per centage) for cutting in 3 yds. wide (with liberty to widen out to 4 yds.), and 2d. per ton extra. If fallen on one side, 1d. per ton extra.

Holeing and removing flooring dirt up to 9 in. in thickness, 1d. per ton extra.

In Stret work: Setting 12 ft. bars 1s. each, 7 ft. bars 5d. each.

Wide work: On end of coal, 2d. per ton extra.

Colliers working in making out places	5/-
Drawers working in making out places	4/-
Men to find explosives.	
Colliers' day wage	3/10
Drawers	3/6

PRICES NOT SUBJECT TO PERCENTAGES.

Crabbing, or pushing up on the dip of the mine, after the first 13 yds., 1d. per ton down to 26 yds., and an additional 1d. per ton for every 10 yds. afterwards.

Long Drawing.—Where drawing exceeds 150 yds. on level, 1d. per ton extra up to 200 yards, and 1d. per ton for every additional 50 yds.

Where drawing exceeds 100 yds. up brow, 1d. per ton extra, and 1d. per ton for every additional 50 yds. over 100 yards.

Filling tanks with water, 3d. per small tank, and 6d. per large tank.

Filling and emptying boxes with dirt, 8d. per box including drawing, if beyond drawing limit 1d. per box extra; 4d. per box if filled only; emptied only, 4d. per box

Setting 7 ft. bars, 5d. per bar.

Setting prop chocks 4 ft. 6 in. square, filled with dirt, 3s. 6d. each, and prop chocks 4 ft. 6 in. high to be paid in like proportion.

Drawing props, 1d. per prop.

Half-end and face places to be paid half-end and face prices.

PRICES FOR COAL GETTING AS IN 1888 (Mr. Simm)

THE PRINCESS PIT RESCUE TEAM (Mr. Maddison)

Haydock, a single woman aged 22 years, of Copperhouse Row, Ashton-in-Makerfield was killed by a locomotive as she was walking up the lines. She did not hear the engine and was run over.

The driver did not whistle and the brakesman was between the two coal waggons although he stated that he was watching but did not see her until she was between the wheels.

From 'THE REPORT OF THE MINES INSPECTOR'.
6th. November 1900.

Arthur Thorpe aged 18 years, a haulage hand was killed whilst lowering some tubs. He got in front and they overpowered him through some men pushing at his request. He was crushed against the stationary tubs and died on the 19th. in Haydock Cottage Hospital.

From 'THE NEWTON AND EARLESTOWN GUARDIAN'.
17th. May 1901.

CORONER BRIGHOUSE AND

HAYDOCK COTTAGE HOSPITAL.

At the inquest on the body of John McGee aged 14 years, son of Patrick who lived in Juddfield Street, Haydock, it was heard that the deceased was helping some men to empty bricks from tubs near an angle wheel and the rope was in motion. He was caught by the wheel and his skull was fractured. The accident was not seen and he was taken to the hospital and died later.

Nurse Jack, the sister at the hospital, was questioned and asked for a statement that McGee might have made in hospital. She had asked him how the accident happened but he had made no reply.

The jury returned a verdict 'Accidental Death' and the coroner stated that he and the jury had been discussing another matter relating to the death on how the Haydock Hospital was supported and was told that it was supported by an Honorary Committee.

From 'THE NEWTON AND EARLESTOWN GUARDIAN'.
18th. March 1904.

HAYDOCK COLLIERY SICK CLUB.

Michael McDonald, 222, Liverpool Road, Pewfall, Haydock, made a claim at the St Helens County Court under the Workman's Compensation Act.

He was employed at Princess pit and on the 28th. December 1903 was descending the cage when it was suddenly brought to a stop with a jerk and he hurt his knee.

Compensation had been paid but it was alleged that four weeks payment had not been received. Mr John Robinson, General Manager for Richard Evans and Company, said under the rules of the Sick Club that workman should allow the payments to be deducted from this payments and this had not been done, so he forthwith ceased to be a member of the Club.

The Judge allowed the man to pay the money to the Club and he was awarded £1 a week from the 12th. January.

Mr. Riley asked for costs on a higher scale because this effected some 5000 workmen who were employed and this had been brought as a test case. The judge declined to award costs on the higher scale.

From **'THE NEWTON AND EARLESTOWN GUARDIAN'**.
31st. March 1905.
EARLESTOWN COLLIER KILLED.

At the inquest into the death of John Champion of Vista Road Earlestown by Mr. Brighouse in St. Helens who was killed. at about 6 pm. on Friday.

The deceased was working with Simon Ratcliffe in the Little Delph Mine. The fireman visited the place and after giving certain instructions left them roofing down. Everything seemed to be safe. About 8 pm. the fireman heard the fall and found the deceased completely covered. Ratcliffe was at the other side of the fall and escaped.

Mr. Owen, the fireman, said he gave instructions to take out a bar and put another in it's place. Contrary to instructions the deceased rolled the first bar off and left it to do something to the second bar but did not set another in the place of the first.

Ratcliffe said he heard the roof going and told the deceased. 'I suppose you heard that?'

The deceased replied that he could and went away a few yards. All was quiet for some time and they commenced work again. The deceased was going back to the leg of the second prop when the fall occurred.

Mr. Robinson, the Manager, said he had always found the man a good workman and he was surprised that he had acted as Ratcliffe said.

John Cawfield, a youth, stated he saw him knock out the second bar. Verdict 'accidental death'.

The deceased was a Cornishman and came from St. Ives to Earlestown two years ago. He was a member of the Salvation Army in both towns. On Tuesday he had walked 20 miles collecting for the 'Self Denial Fund'. The funeral took place at Parr and was conducted by Captain Green. The deceased was accorded full Salvation Army honours.

From **'THE REPORT OF THE MINES INSPECTOR'**.
23rd. September 1908.

John Davies aged 58 years, a dataller, was travelling down the self acting endless rope brow and was found crushed by a full tub against a low bar.

It probably happened when he reached over to the electric signal to move the tubs which would have been opposite each other. At the enquiry it was advised to enlarge the brow.

From **'THE ST.HELENS REPORTER'**.
15th. December 1916.
COLLIERS DEATH.

John Smith of 46, Clipsley Lane died in Haydock Cottage Hospital from injuries received on Sunday night at work in the Princess pit of Messrs. Richard Evans and Co. He leaves a widow and two children.

The Lancashire and Cheshire Coal Owners financed a Rescue Station at Boothstown and soon afterwards each colliery had it's owned trained team. The men were trained in the use of the 'Proto' breathing apparatus.

The men of the Princess Colliery Rescue Team are pictured with the apparatus and a collection of miners lamps.

The cage is for the canary that was used to test for gas and only went out of use in collieries in 1985.

From **'THE NEWTON AND EARLESTOWN GUARDIAN'**.
9th. November 1917.
HAYDOCK COLLIERY MANAGER KILLED.

Mr. Roger Banks, the Manager at Princess pit, was killed in the mine on Sunday afternoon when he was getting into the wrong deck of the cage and was so badly crushed that he died before he could be taken to the surface.

Before the First World War a German company built a factory in Haydock to manufacture brickettes from the small coal and coal dust. At the out break of the Great War, the Germans were interned and the business stopped but the building stood for many years and was known as 'Schwartz Kop'.

Richard Evans and Company used it as a stores and at one time it was the headquarters of the Princess Pit Rescue team.

The pile of bricks in the foreground are believed to be the Queen pit chimney which had been demolished shortly before the picture was taken.

QUEEN COLLIERY

The colliery was situated near the Offices of Richard Evans and Co. in Haydock and close to King, Princess and Legh pits.

On the 26th. December 1868 twenty six men and boys lost their lives in an explosion of firedamp at the colliery. Of the men in the mine at the time, only one, Hugh Arnold escaped with his life although he was injured.

The village was recovering from this shattering experience when another explosion took place in the same mine on the 21st. July 1869, when Joseph Edwards and fifty six others lost their lives in an explosion of firedamp.

From **'THE INSPECTOR OF MINES REPORT'**.
1st. September 1877.

Tryphena Harrison aged 25 years, a browman, was killed when she fell down the pit from the surface.

From **'THE INSPECTOR OF MINES REPORT'**.
9th. July 1886.

Mary Brichall aged 39 years, a pit brow girl, was killed when the waggoner was lowering a waggon down to the next screen.

SCHWARTZ KOP (Mr. Bond)

The deceased, who was in the waggon, was crushed against the screen shute.

She had been told by the waggonman that a waggon was to be lowered but she must have been taken by surprise as she could easily have slipped into the side of the shute.

From 'THE INSPECTOR OF MINES REPORT'.
4th. July 1887.

Isiah Davies aged 14 years, a pony driver. The lad was in charge of a pony taking full tubs up the brow and it is supposed that the gearing gave way letting the tub run back onto him. There should have been a drag chain on the tub but he did not use it.

As the collieries closed, the features that had become part of the landscape were demolished.

RAINFORD COLLIERIES

There have been many collieries in the Rainford area. The Rainford Colliery was situated one mile south of Rainford Junction and is mentioned in the Victorian Inspector's Reports. In 1894 it employed 580 people and had two groups of collieries Nos. 1 and 2 and Nos. 3 and 4. For many years the colliery was owned by the Rainford Coal Co. but when it closed in 1928 it was under the ownership of Bromilow Foster and Co.

FELLING THE CHIMNEY AT QUEEN COLLIERY (Mr. Simm)

From 'THE PRESCOT REPORTER'.
19th. MAY 1860.

Henry Evans collier was caught in a fall of roof at the colliery owned by the Moss Hall Coal Company and is in a precarious state.

The picks, crow bars and shovels which were the tools of the collier belonged to him and he had to purchase and take care of them. They were usually left locked up down the pit when the collier finished work and it was a serious offence for them to be stolen.

From 'THE ST.HELENS STANDARD'.
1st. August 1865.
STEALING COLLIERS PICKS.

At the Police Court in St.Helens on Monday Mr.James Leadbetter, a collier in the employ of Messrs. Harding at Rainford was brought into custody charged with stealing a pick, the property of Richard Rothwell and another charge of stealing a pick belonging to Henry Kenyon.

Mr. Marsh defended, and in the first case a witness said that he worked in the No. 8 pit. He was engaged about three weeks ago when he lost a pick. He left it in the usual place and found it in the possession of the defendant. The pick was identified in court as the property of Rothwell. On being charged the defendant said that it was a mistake.

The second charge was then taken and Henry Kenyon said that he missed the pick from where it was usually left. It was found along with other picks in the engine room.

Mr. Marsh examined the prisoner at some length. The underlooker was called and he said that the prisoner identified all the picks in the engine room as his.

P.C. Shaw charged Leadbetter with the theft of the picks and he was committed for trial at the Sessions and released on bail.

From 'THE WIGAN OBSERVER'
29th. April 1865.

On Saturday at the colliery owned by Harding and Co., Henry Cotton aged 42 years, a collier, was working with his son Peter in the No. 7 pit when a large quantity of coal fell on them. The inquest was held on Monday at the Rainford Junction Hotel, when a verdict of accidental death was recorded.

From 'THE ST.HELENS STANDARD'.
14th. July 1865.

THE LANCASHIRE COALFIELD.

XXII.—Rainford Collieries.

This property is situated about one mile south of Rainford Junction on the Lancashire and Yorkshire Railway, and eleven miles north-east of Liverpool. The lessees of the collieries are the Rainford Coal Company Limited, Mr. George Boole being the general manager. Two distinct plants are in operation—viz., Rainford Nos. 1 and 2; and Rainford Nos. 3 and 4, about 200 yards distant from the former. At each plant a steam hauling engine is placed at the top of the winding shaft to haul coal up the main downbrow underground, by means of plough steel endless ropes; and beyond the downbrow, motors actuated by compressed air are largely used for hauling coal and working pumps. Each colliery is provided with a Schiele fan for ventilating purposes. Two large air-compressors are placed on the surface near No. 2 shaft, and the compressed air is conveyed in pipes to both collieries for the work referred to above; by this motive-power a considerable part of the underground haulage is performed.

Rainford Nos. 1 and 2 Shafts.

The shafts are 40 yards apart in an east and west line, the dip being nearly west. The winding engine is placed between the shafts, and one of the ropes winds coal from No. 2 or downcast, while the other rope runs a cage and balance weight in No. 1 or upcast; the cage in the latter is utilised for lowering and raising the workmen. No. 2 shaft is 11 ft. diameter and 160 yards in depth to the seven-feet or Lindsay seam, and No. 1 is 9½ ft. diameter and of the same depth.

Winding.—The winding engine has two horizontal cylinders, 24 in. by 54 in. ordinary slide-valves, and drums for flat ropes 13 ft. diameter at first lift. It raises four tubs of 8 cwt. capacity on two decks in the cage in No. 2 shaft; the conductors are of pitch pine, two to a cage, one at each end.

Water Lifting.—The pumping engine, on the surface, has one horizontal cylinder, 24 in. by 54 in., geared 1 to 4, with two horizontal connecting rods, working to two quadrants placed over No. 2 shaft. It raises water from the depth of 169 yards (sump inclusive) in two bucket lifts, one designed to balance the other to a great extent. The top lift has 15¾ in. bucket, 5 ft. stroke, 97 yards in length, and the bottom lift 15⅜ in. bucket, 5 ft. stroke, raising water 72 yards to a lodge room at that depth. It is in operation eighteen hours per day, at the rate of six strokes per minute, and when in good order will deliver 228 gallons to the surface per minute

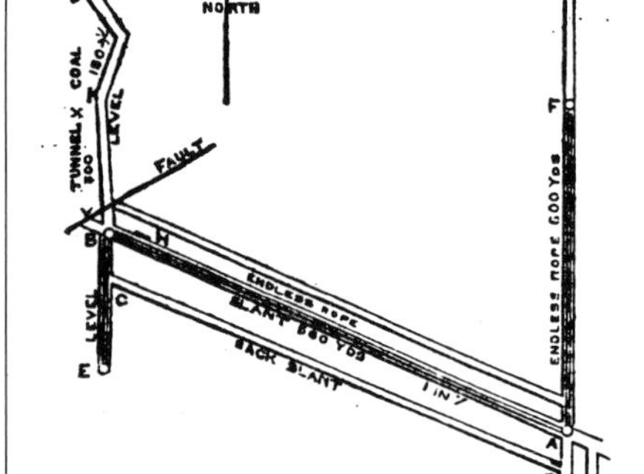

Underground Hauling.—The engine for this purpose is also placed at the surface. It has two horizontal cylinders, 16 in. by 30 in., geared 1 to 12. On the third-motion shaft of this engine a five-grooved driving pulley, 6 ft. in diameter, is keyed. The rope is of plough steel, 1 in. diameter, made on Lang's lay principle, and is taken four and a-half turns round the driving pulley. At 25 ft. forward another steel shaft is placed, having four single-grooved pulleys running loose upon it. By passing the rope four turns over the grooved driving pulley and the four loose pulleys, sufficient grip is obtained to prevent the rope slipping. This arrangement admits of each loose pulley accommodating itself to the wear of the corresponding groove on the driving pulleys, and answers well. When the engine was first started, there was one four-grooved pulley keyed on the front shaft, but the friction and wear of ropes was such that a change was necessitated. Above is given a sketch plan of the underground arrangements in the 7 ft. or Lindsay seam. D is the downcast, U the upcast shaft, A B is the main engine brow. At the point A a 6 in. vertical steel shaft is fixed, on which two C pulleys, 4½ ft. diameter, are placed; these pulleys are fitted with cast iron liners, so as to be readily replaced when worn; the driving rope is taken two and a-half turns around the upper of these pulleys, and from thence to the point B, where another vertical steel shaft is fixed, with similar pulleys to those at A, the driving rope being taken two and a-half turns around the upper pulley, and from there to the tightening pulley at E, and back to the engine. The lower pulley at the vertical shaft at A is loose, but it can be put in or out of gear by an ordinary clutch; as a rule the endless rope passing two and a-half turns around it is kept going to work the plane, A F, a tightening pulley being placed at F. A similar endless rope may be driven from the lower pulley on the vertical shaft, at B, to work the plane B G. The tubs are connected to the endless ropes in couples by lashing chains, both at front and back.

Compressed Air Motors.—One motor in connection with the underground haulage is placed at F. It has two 10 in. by 15 in. cylinders, geared 1 to 4, and two 3 ft. drums for main and tail ropes, working the level beyond the point F. This is a self-contained engine, constructed by Messrs. Wood and Gee, of Wigan, as also the hauling engine on the surface. Another hauling engine is placed at the top of the back slant of 1 in 7 at D; this engine has two 15 in. by 30 in. air cylinders, one 5 ft. drum, and is used for lowering and raising trains of ten tubs each, which are provided for carrying the workmen to and from the bottom of the brow; each tub carries six persons. The rope is of best plough steel, ⅞ in. diameter, and a safety rope is carried through a wood pipe extending the whole length of the train inside each tub, thus forming an attachment at the front as well as the back of the train in case of a coupling failing. There are also five dogs or holders placed under the train in a horizontal position ordinarily, but which can instantly be let down by the train rider should the ropes fail; the holders in this case dig into the floor and sleepers, being prevented from turning over by a link.

The underground pumps are all driven by compressed air. A Pearn vertical pump is placed at the bottom of the downbrow, at H, the motor having two 14 in. cylinders, 10 in. stroke, working two 7 in. rams. Another motor near it has one 16 in. horizontal cylinder, 2 ft. stroke, working a 6½ in. double-acting plunger pump. An Evans Cornish pump, placed at K, has one cylinder, 10 in. by 18 in., driving a 4 in. double-acting plunger pump. A Cameron pump with two 12 in. cylinders, 10 in. stroke and two 4½ in. rams, is placed at the point G. The water pipes on the downbrow are 6 in. diameter. The air pipes on the downbrow from the shaft are 4 in. diameter from the bottom of the downbrow to the north way, at G, 3 in. diameter, and from A to F 2 in. diameter.

Air-Compressors.—These are on the surface, consisting of two 25 in. steam cylinders, 4½ ft. stroke, and two 25 in. air cylinders, each working to the flywheel shaft in line; they were constructed by Messrs. Walker Brothers, of Wigan, in 1874. There are two large receivers at the engine, the pressure being 50 lb. The air is taken down the shaft in 7 in. pipes.

Ventilation.—This is produced by a Schiele fan, 7 ft. in diameter, driven by an engine with one 16 in. horizontal cylinder, 2 ft. stroke, two pulleys and leather belt. The pulleys are 10 ft. and 2 ft. 8 in. in diameter; the engine speed is seventy-five revolutions, and that of the fan 280 revolutions per minute. This fan was guaranteed by the makers to produce 70,000 cubic feet of air per minute, with a water-gauge of 1½ in. to 2 in., and this quantity has generally been exceeded with 1½ in. water-gauge.

Coal Washing.—The rough slack which is produced from the first screening is washed by the trough system. The slack is first taken from the large screens by an elevator to a second screen, on which it is separated into nuts, pea nuts and dust. When thus sized, each is washed separately. The apparatus is capable of washing effectually 200 tons per day. The water discharged at the end of the troughs, after settling, is forced to the trough head by a No. 9 pulsometer, to be used over again.

Boilers.—Five Galloway boilers of steel, 30 ft. by 7 ft., made in 1891, to work up to 60 lb. pressure, and one egg-ended boiler, supply steam; the usual pressure is 50 lb. for the whole. There are also two Lancashire boilers, 28 ft. by 7 ft., at 50 lb. pressure. The sawmill engine has one 18 in. horizontal cylinder, and is supplied with steam by a Cornish boiler at 40 lb. pressure.

At No. 2 shaft the Galloway and Lancashire boilers are fed by an exhaust steam injector, the feed-water being heated to about 180 degs. Fahr. by the exhaust steam from the air-compressing engines. The water supplied to the boilers is first used for slack washing, and afterwards run into a large reservoir, from whence it is pumped to feed the boilers. It is found that this water is much better for the boilers than it was originally, before slack washing was introduced at the colliery, the deleterious properties in the water seeming to be neutralised in the washing process.

Rainford Nos. 3 and 4 Shafts.

Two shafts are sunk here; No. 3 is the downcast, 11 ft. in diameter, 200 yards in depth to the Arley Mine. No. 4, in proximity, is the winding and upcast shaft, 12 ft. in diameter, of the same depth.

The winding engine at No. 4 shaft has two horizontal cylinders, 11 in. by 30 in., ordinary slide valves, 9 ft. cylindrical drum. The winding ropes are of patent steel, 1 in. in diameter. The conductors are of wire rope, three to a cage, each rope weighted at bottom. Two tubs of 5 cwt. capacity are raised in each cage on one deck. The winding engine at No. 3 shaft has two horizontal cylinders, of 20 in. by 36 in., 13 ft. verticals for flat ropes, two conductors to a cage. The cages are similar to those in No. 3, but at present are not in use.

Hauling.—An engine with one horizontal cylinder, 18 in. by 36 in., geared 1 to 4, is placed at the top of No. 4 shaft. On the second motion shaft the driving five-grooved pulley is keyed, the power being transmitted down to the bottom in the Arley mine by arrangements similar to those at No. 2 shaft. The main downbrow, dipping 1 in 8 to the west, terminates 520 yards west of No. 4 shaft, but the endless-rope haulage system in connection with it extends only 420 yards. Up the brow—on the remaining 100 yards—owing to a fault, the road dips in the contrary direction, and the coal is conveyed to the shaft by a self-acting incline, in sets of sixteen tubs. There are two extensions of the endless-rope haulage in the same direction (west), worked by compressed-air motors. No. 1 has two 6 in. cylinders, 12 in. stroke, geared 1 to 4, one 2½ ft. drum, length of haulage about 400 yards; the empty tubs run down by gravity, and the full tubs are hauled out in sets of nine at once. No. 2 motor, placed at the end of No. 1 road, has two horizontal cylinders, 6 in. by 12 in., geared 1 to 3, one drum 2½ ft. diameter; the empty tubs run down by gravity as above. No. 3 motor works the north level, commencing at the bottom of the endless-rope haulage. It has two horizontal cylinders, 8 in. by 12, geared 1 to 4, and two drums 2½ ft. This level is worked by main and tail ropes over 450 yards. At the bottom of the endless-rope haulage an Evans Cornish pump is placed. The motor has one cylinder, 10 in. by 12 in. stroke, working a double-acting plunger pump, 3 in. diameter, forcing water through 3 in. pipes to the top of the brow. The air pipes in No. 4 shaft are 6 in. diameter, 4 in. diameter to the top of the main brow, and two ranges of 3 in. pipes from the top to bottom of the brow.

Ventilation.—This is produced by a Schiele fan, 9½ ft. in diameter, driven by one horizontal engine, 18 in. cylinder, 2 ft. stroke, the speed of the engine being 79 revolutions, that of the fan 220 revolutions per minute. The fan circulates about 100,000 cubic feet of air per minute through the workings of the Arley mine, under 1¼ in. water-gauge.

Boilers.—There are four egg-ended boilers, three of which are 32 ft. by 5 ft., and one 36 ft. by 5 ft., the working pressure being 50 lb.

Mode of Working.—The Arley mine is got by longwall, the gateways are driven from the rise crossgates on the level course and 15 yards apart; in this direction the work is against the cleavage. The coals are let down the jig brow or crossgate by a balance, as described in Art. xxi. The crossgate cuts off the gateways every 60 yards. The main levels are about 100 yards apart. The seven-feet seam is worked by the bord-and-pillar method, the pillars having been made 20 yards square, but the more modern practice is to make them 30 to 40 yards square, and when worked back a face of several pillars in breadth can be brought away at once, if the conditions of roof and floor admit of this being done. Safety lamps are used exclusively in both mines, the Marsaut and Mueseler lamps being used by the miners, and Mr. Hall's lamp by the firemen. The explosive used is roburite, both for coal in narrow work and stone work; the shots are fired at night by the shot-lighter, when the hewers are all out of the mines.

Jig Brows.—Several self-acting inclines or jig brows are in operation in both mines. The principal points of interest in these is that the jig wheel is vertical, and two roads are used; the full tubs always descend on the same road on one side, and the empty tubs ascend on the other side, so that the siding arrangements at top and bottom are more convenient.

On all main hauling roads electric signals are in use for communicating with the enginemen and the different shunts on the roads. All main roads are laid with steel rails of T section, 18 lb. per yard, and fish-plated at the joints.

On the large stationary engines solidified oil and Stauffer lubricators are used for the bearings, and sight-feed lubricators are adopted for the cylinders.

M. E.

The consumption of coal in Hamburg, according to the yearly report of Messrs. B. Blumenfeld of that town, diminished from 2,708,250 tons in 1891 to 2,518,185 tons in 1892.

EXCERPT FROM THE COLLIERY GUARDIAN (Wigan Reference Library)

CROSSING AT CROSS PIT LANE, RAINFORD (St.HLH&AL)

On Saturday morning an accident occurred at the colliery owned by Thomas Wallays to a boy named Charles Birch, aged 13 years, the son of James Birch a brickmaker of Dentons Green. He was a drawer in the Rushy Park Mine and was working, when a portion of the roof fell on him. On removing the debris it was found that he was quite dead.

The inquest was held at the house of Mr. Littler in Dentons Green on Monday and returned a verdict of accidental death.

From *'THE ST.HELENS STANDARD'*
29th. May 1869.

An inquest was held at the Wheatsheaf Inn in Rainford into the death of William Lee aged 55 years who was a waggon greaser at the Rainford Coal Co.

He was seen on Friday leaning against a waggon and he was later found between the buffers and it is supposed that the poor fellow was unable to get out of the way in time. Verdict accidental death.

There was an explosion at the colliery on 10th. January 1869, which resulted in the deaths of nine men and set fire to the coal underground.

From *'THE ST.HELENS STANDARD'*.
30th. January 1869.
THE RAINFORD COLLIERY EXPLOSION.

On Saturday the fire was extinguished and the bodies of Whalley and Burrows were found and brought to the surface. It seems strange to say that they were in a good state of preservation. Burrows was black and there was debris on him but he was little disfigured.

Colliers were responsible for buying and storing their own explosives for use at their work. The explosive used at this time was gunpowder. The following is a cautionary tale.

From *'THE ST.HELENS STANDARD'*.
3rd. April 1875.
DRUNKEN FATE OF COLLIER.

James Lackland went to the home of another collier in Skelmersdale when he was drunk. James Howard had four children and could not light the fire. Lackland, having three pounds of gunpowder with him, threw a handful onto the fire, which wrecked the house and severely burnt all that were in. Lackland was taken into custody.

As the collieries grew, St.Helens and the surrounding district was criss-crossed with branch lines for the transportation of the coal. There were many level-crossings which have all now disappeared.

During the 1921 and the 1926 Strikes in the coal industry, many people went picking coal on the waste tips around the area to supplement their income.

RAVENHEAD COLLIERY

The colliery was situated on Burtonhead Road, opposite the Phoenix Colliery. There has been coal mined in the Ravenhead area since the 1760's, when John Mackay, the Scottish industrialist, started mining operations. He owned collieries in Thatto Heath,

COALPICKERS DURING 1921 STRIKE (St.HLH&AL)

THE HEADGEARS OF RAVENHEAD COLLIERY (SMM)

Parr and Ravenhead, and was one of the men who greatly influenced the development of St. Helens. A series of seams were named after the Ravenhead area, where they outcropped. In the nineteenth century the area was mined by Messrs. Bromilow and Haddock, with a production in the 1860's of 150,000 tons of coal per year.

The modern colliery was sunk to a depth of 540 yards in 1866, and then in 1876, the colliery merged with the St. Helens Colliery to form the St. Helens Collieries Co. Ltd. At the turn of the century the manpower was in the region of 700 men.

After nationalisation, the colliery was producing 260,000 tons of coal per year, with a workforce of about 1,000 men. Ravenhead Colliery closed in October 1968, when it was producing 207,000 tons of coal with a workforce of 500 men.

From 'THE WIGAN OBSERVER'
5th. February 1854

James Rigby, a stoker, was crushed by one of the engines. At the inquest into his death it was stated that he was oiling the engine while it was at work and he was struck on the head and killed.

From 'THE WIGAN OBSERVER.'
22nd. September 1855.

Nathaniel Mills, Peter Fyldes, Edward Gerard and Philip Masterson were brought before the magistrates charged with stealing a large quantity of brass.

John Cartwright, the store keeper at Bromilow's Foundry said he purchased 23 pounds, of brass from the prisoners and found later it was stolen. It had come from the Ravenhead Colliery and was part of a much larger quantity stolen on the morning of the 27th. when the store was broken into. They were all committed for trial at the next Kirkdale Sessions.

From 'THE REPORT OF THE MINES INSPECTOR'.
1st. October 1863.

George Billange aged 20 years, an unemployed drawer, was killed when one of the three boilers at the colliery, of a haycock shape and had been in use for over a quarter of a century, burst, causing the death of the poor fellow who was in search of employment at the colliery and had taken shelter in the boiler house.

The boiler burst from over pressure and

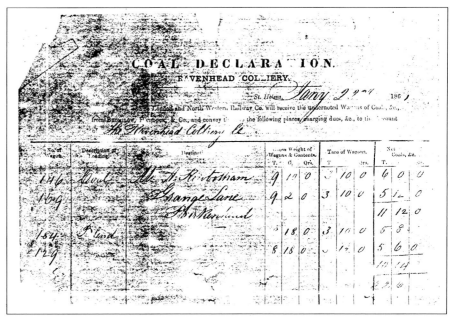

COAL DECLARATION (Mr. Atherton)

parts of it had been repaired and the boiler maker had reported it fit for work. He must have neglected to examine several plates near the bottom which appeared to the Inspector to not exceed the thickness of a shilling.

From 'THE COLLIERY GUARDIAN'.
14th. November 1863.

A considerable amount of damage was done by overwinding the engine at Groves Colliery but there was no loss of life or injury to any person. The amount of damage was put at £200.

Steam was got up about 3.30 pm. in the temporary absence of the engineer and the engine started. Before it could be stopped, the cage had come into contact with the headgear causing the damage.

From 'THE ST.HELENS STANDARD'.
24th. February 1866.

An accident occurred at the colliery on Tuesday the 13th., when Thomas Radcliffe who lived in Waterloo Street was killed.

It appears that he was about 67 years old and employed as a blacksmith at the colliery for only a short time as he had been out of work for a long time.

On the day in question he was engaged with others in making alterations to the headgear, in the course of which, it was necessary to take a rope round a capstan and to a height of forty feet on a set of shears and then pull it down the other side.

Two men named Handley and Gillibrand were working with him and the rope became stiff and they could not move it. Handley got the idea of attaching the rope to the beam of the steam engine which was

raising and falling eight feet. They thought that they could get the engine to do what they could not do.

The first attempt to attach the rope failed but on the second attempt he was more successful. The rope was immediately pulled down and the capstan handle whirred round knocking off the men at the top.

The men that had not been injured lifted Radcliffe to the carpenters shop and then assisted him to walk home when it was found that he had injured various parts of his body and was complaining about an ache in his neck. He took to bed and became dangerously ill and expired on Tuesday night.

At the inquest at Mr. Leyland's Angel Inn in Barrow Street a verdict of 'accidental death' was returned.

From 'THE ST.HELENS STANDARD'.
19th February 1870.

Margaret Ryan, a middle aged Irish woman, was charged with stealing twenty four pounds of coal from Groves colliery at Sutton.

Joseph Heyes, the overlooker at the pit, said at 8.15 he saw her on a coal waggon taking coal .She ran away but he caught her. She told him it was a very small piece of coal. She said to the Bench that her husband had been out of work since Christmas and she took the coal to make the children warm. There was nothing against the woman's character and the Bench sent her to jail for seven days.

In the 1921 Coal Strike coal picking went on at the colliery tips.

COAL PICKING (Mrs. Lesham)

Pigeon House Mine.

HAND GOT COAL.

(1) For getting and filling hand-got coal into boxes and drawing to the haulage, including the setting of face timber. Explosives Free   per ton 3/9

(2) Strait up to 10 feet wide on end   .... per yard 4/7½

     Strait up to 10 feet wide on face .... per yard 3/3½

     Ribbing past a fall on the working face ...... Half strait price

(3) When the collier is required to set bars on the face .... per bar 4d.

(4) When a collier has worked part of a shift getting coal in his own working place and he is required to do work other than coal getting coal for the remaining part of that shift he shall be paid at the rate of the collier's daywage of 9/11 per shift for the remaining part of the shift. When he is required to work a full shift in work other than getting coal he shall be paid as provided for in the County Agreement.

(5) In the event of a collier or drawer failing to earn the collier's or drawer's daywage on the average over the number of days worked in any week he shall be made up to the collier's or drawer's daywage respectively ......

(6) Prices and conditions for other work to be as specified in the General Price List ....

WAGES FOR HAND GOT COAL (Mr. McGuirk)

During the years of the Great Depression in the 1930's, work was scarce as collieries worked on 'short time'. The photograph was taken between 1933-5. The man with the shovel is Harry Lesley Tickle but the other man is not named.

From **'THE NEWTON AND EARLESTOWN GUARDIAN'.**
24th. January 1930.
ST. HELENS COLLIERY TRAGEDY.

A verdict of 'misadventure' was returned on David Owen Williams of 32 Taylor Street Sutton who was killed at the mine on Friday. Henry Pheasant of Sandy Lane, Skelmersdale said he was working three yards away from Williams when a piece of coal on which they were working suddenly fell out of the roof pushing the witness on one side and came to rest on the deceased with his head pressed to his chest.

Colliers who could find steady work in the 1930's were few and when they could find work they did not earn a lot. The wage agreement for the colliery has survived from 1938.

The Coal Board installed boot cleaners at the colliery for the use of the workforce.

COLLIERS WORKING UNDERGROUND (Mrs. M. Wilson)

Pigeon House Seam.

PRICE LIST.

HAND GOT COAL LOADED ON TO CONVEYOR.

(1) To filling hand-got coal on to conveyor, including propping and barring. The necessary timber to be supplied to the colliers at the point required on the face. Explosives Free ......   per ton 3/1

(2) In the event of the coal having to be thrown out before being filled on to conveyor—extra payment shall be made by mutual arrangement with the men on the face ......

(3) Should a difficulty occur on the face—steps, rolls, broken roof, etc.—which interferes with the filling of the coal on to conveyor, extra payment shall be made by mutual arrangement with the men on the face.

(4) Payment for other work—ribbing and strait work, setting chocks, withdrawing timber, following dirt, etc., shall be made in accordance with the General Price List.

(5) In the event of the colliers failing to earn at the above prices the daywage rate as set out in Clause (1) of the Agreement of the 25th October, 1934, it is agreed by the Company to make them up to that amount.

WAGES FOR COAL LOADED TO CONVEYOR (Mr. McGuirk)

LANCASHIRE AND CHESHIRE COAL INDUSTRY.

Wages Agreement dated 9th May, 1938.

List of Rates for various Classes of Workpeople.

GRADE	Basis Rates 1938 s. d.	Minimum 6% on Basis s. d.	Flat Rate Advance s. d.	Total s. d.
Collier (Minimum)	8 7	9 1	1 0	10 1
Collier (Daywage)	9 11	10 6	1 0	11 6
Drawer (Sharing) over 21	7 11	8 5	1 0	9 5
Drawer (Sharing) between 20 and 21				
Dataller	7 7	8 0	0 6	8 6
Shotlighter	7 9	8 3	1 0	9 3
Electrician (Underground)	9 11	10 6	1 0	11 6
Rope Splicer	7 9	8 3	1 0	9 3
Onsetter 1st Man	7 9	8 3	1 0	9 3
" 2nd Man	7 9	8 3	1 0	9 3
Pusher-on	7 9	8 3	1 0	9 3
Enginemen (Underground)	7 9	8 3	1 0	9 3
Leading Banksman	7 9	8 3	1 0	9 3
Second "	7 7	8 0	1 0	9 0
Sinkers Grade 1	8 7	9 1	1 0	10 1
" Grade 2	7 11	8 5	1 0	9 5
" Grade 3	7 9	8 3	1 0	9 3
Machine & Pan Faces.				
Scufter	8 7	9 1	1 0	10 1
Pan & Belt Shifter, Grade 1	8 7	9 1	1 0	10 1
" " Grade 2	8 3	8 9	1 0	9 9
Packers	8 7	9 1	1 0	10 1
Timbermen (accompanying Machine)	8 7	9 1	1 0	10 1

WAGES AGREEMENT FROM MAY 1938 (Mr. McGuirk)

SITE OF RAVENHEAD OPENCAST (Mr. Davis)

PILLAR AND STALL WORKING AT RAVENHEAD OPENCAST (Mr. Davis)

RED GATE COLLIERY

The colliery was situated halfway to Boardman's Lane. There was a colliery mentioned in this area in the 'Inspector's Report' for 1873, when George Molyneux worked it. It was sold in 1883 and reputedly closed in 1884.

From **'THE REPORT ON THE INSPECTOR OF MINES.**
6th. November 1891.
James Doolan aged 40 years, a sinker, was killed at 2 am. in the 4th. hour of the shift when a piece of band fell from the side of the pit and hit him on the head. The bricking was 10 yards from the bottom and the place had been reported safe.

ROYAL COLLIERY

There are two collieries called 'Royal' on record in the town.
ROYAL 1. (Bird in'th Hand), which was situated at the corner of Prescot Road and Grosvenor Road, close to the Toll Bar, where David Bromilow & Co. mined the Rushy Park Seam in the 1830's. The colliery was closed in about 1861.

ROYAL 2, which was situated on French Street. The workings of this colliery were reopened by John Cross in 1875, probably by a different shaft. It closed in 1879.

From **'THE REPORT OF THE MINES INSPECTOR.**
6th. February 1851.
It was reported that John Turton was killed by falling down the shaft.

From **'THE REPORT OF THE MINES INSPECTOR'.**
8th. June 1864.
The two children, John Sweeny aged 8 years and Edward Price aged 6 years were playing with other children about the pit top which was covered with planks, when by some means unexplained, the planks were removed and the lads fell to their deaths.

RUSHY PARK COLLIERY

The colliery was situated between Glade Hill Colliery and the railway line,

near Island's Brow. This colliery was first referred to in 1801, when a group of salt proprietors purchased a thirty year lease to mine coal. Bromilow and Sothern owned the colliery in the 1830's and 1840's.

SANKEYBROOK COLLIERY

This was situated on Redgate Drive and was already established by the 1840's. It was mentioned in the 'Inspector's Reports' for 1850 and 1855, as being owned by the Sankey Brook Colliery Co. In in 1862, the recorded production was 100,000 tons of coal per year. It was later merged with the Ashton Green Colliery to form the Sankey Coal Co. Ltd., but this concern was not successful, and folded in 1869. The last reference to the colliery is in 1873, when it was owned by Henry Bramall & Co., of St. Helens. The colliery probably closed around 1876.

From **'THE REPORT OF THE INSPECTOR OF MINES'.**
5th. December 1850.
Thomas Briscoe was killed by a fall of roof.

From **'THE WIGAN EXAMINER'.**
20th. April 1866.
FATAL ACCIDENT.
On Tuesday a boy named William Kelsall aged 12 years, son of Ann Kelsall of Peasley Cross, was accidentally killed at the

Sankey Brook Colliery whilst engaged in the cleaning of a portion of the machinery connected to the engine. His head was nearly severed from his body.

From **'THE REPORT OF THE INSPECTOR OF MINES'.**
5th. July 1865.
Ann Highcock aged 19 years, a coal drawer was killed by falling from one stage to another along with the coal boxes she was pushing. She fell about seven feet.

SENELEY GREEN COLLIERY

From **'THE REPORT OF THE INSPECTOR OF MINES'.**
29th. May 1857.
Thomas Gomer, a drawer, was killed by a fall of roof.

From **'THE REPORT OF THE INSPECTOR OF MINES'.**
13th. November 1857.
John Fryer a drawer was killed by a fall of roof and coal.

SHALEY BROW COLLIERY

From **'THE REPORT OF THE INSPECTOR OF MINES'.**
22nd. October 1852.
John Clarkson was killed when a tub of coal was being loaded and fell down the pit on him as he was preparing to ascend.

COAL DECLARATION 1861 (Mr. Atherton)

SHERDLEY COLLIERY

This colliery was situated on Broadgate Avenue. It first appeared in the 'Inspector's Report' for 1873, with two pits being listed. At that time, it was worked by Bournes and Robinson, who mined extensively in St. Helens in the nineteenth century. During the 1880's the colliery was purchased by the Whitecross Co. Ltd. of Warrington, and in the 1890's the manpower was over 500 men.

From *'THE REPORT OF THE MINES INSPECTOR'*.
9th. January 1874.

John Glynn aged 37 years, a collier who was crushed by a stone in the Main Delf Mine.

From *'THE REPORT OF THE MINES INSPECTOR'*.
27th. April 1894.

James Cliff aged 15 years a pony driver was killed at 12.20 pm in the 7th. hour of the shift. While waiting for full tubs near the face, a layer of coal and shale fell from the slip, carrying a prop and crushing the deceased.

Contractors were employed to do the servicing work in a mine. They were paid by the colliery company and they, in turn, paid the men they employed.

THE HEADGEARS AT SHERDLEY COLLIERY (Mr. Simm)

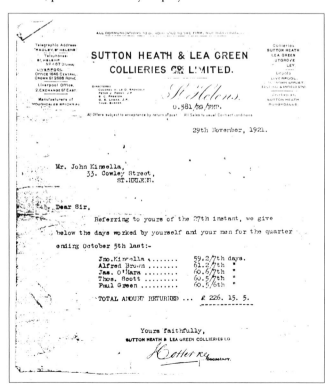

THE EARNINGS OF JOHN KINSELLA IN THE YARD MINE (Mrs. Lever)

Many people will remember the old headgears that stood for a long time after the colliery ceased to work.

The water that was pumped out of the colliery was used for cooling purposes at the United Glass factory. This went on even after the colliery closed. No water is taken from underground now but the surface water from the colliery site is used for the sprinkler system at the factory.

STANLEY COLLIERY

Situated at the end of Old Nook Lane. This colliery was reputed to have been purchased by Bromilow and Sothern from John and William Stock in 1849. Although it does not appear in the Inspector's Reports for 1850 and 1855, it does appear in 1873, under their name. The colliery does not appear in the 1888 report.

ST. HELENS COLLIERY

This colliery was situated between Watson Street and the canal. It was first recorded in the 'Hardshaw Colliery Letter Book' for 1805. It was put up for sale in 1844, due to a coal recession. It was later purchased in 1857, by the Pilkington Brothers, the glass manufacturers. In the 1860's it was producing 130,000 tons of coal per year. From that time onwards it was referred to as the 'Cropdeep' or 'Crop and Deep' pits. The Alexandra shaft was sunk very close to the shafts of these collieries, probably being part of the same work. The last official report was the 'Inspector's Report' of 1894, which lists both 'Alexandra', 'Crop and Deep pits', with the same manager, but no men listed as working there.

From *'THE REPORT OF THE MINES INSPECTOR'*.

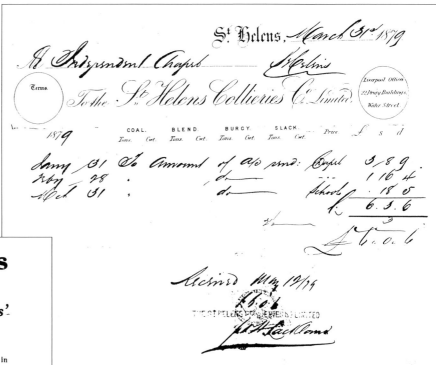

PAPER HEADING (St.HLH&AL)

The photograph dates from about 1920 and shows the surface workers at the colliery. The group includes Teresa Turton.

STOCKS COLLIERY

This was situated off Church Road, Haydock near the border with Ashton-in-Makerfield. It was worked by the Legh family in the eighteenth century,

the coal being sold mostly as land sale.

STRIKES

THE GENERAL STRIKE OF 1926

1926 was a notable year in the country's history. There had been unrest in the mining industry for some time. On Saturday 1st. May, the T.U.C. Conference approved a plan for a National Strike in support of the miners by 3,653,527 votes for to 49,911 votes against.

Headlines in the *'REPORTER'*

Miners' Wages
IN LANCASHIRE AND CHESHIRE.

What does the Coal Owners' Offer mean?

IT MEANS :-

1. Every man, woman and boy will receive an increase in wages.

2. The amount of increase for the four main classes will be as follows :

Surface (Adult)	6s. 6d.	will become 7s. 6½d. per shift.
Haulage (Adult)........	7s. 7½d.	,, ,, 8s. 6½d. ,, ,,
Day wagemen	7s. 9d.	,, ,, 8s. 9d. ,, ,,
Coal getter (minimum)	8s. 7d.	,, ,, 9s. 5½d. ,, ,,

3. (a) The subsistence level will be raised from 7s. 9d. per day to 8s. 9d. per day and the allowance from 1s. to 1s. 1½d. per day.

   (b) The general minimum will be raised from 20 per cent. to 32½ per cent. over 1914 rates (including any adjustments thereof), whilst the lowest paid day-wage workmen will be advanced to 40 per cent. over 1914 rates, and the adult haulage hand specially advanced to the figure shown in the table above.

4. As the amount the Owners are entitled to will be reduced from 17 per cent. to 15 per cent. upon the standard wages and to 13 per cent. of the surplus, the workers in the industry will benefit to a greater extent in the proceeds, and wages will increase more quickly when selling prices advance.

5. This increase in wages represents an addition of about £1,750,000 per annum payable to the workers in Lancashire and Cheshire.

THOS. R. RATCLIFFE-ELLIS,
SECRETARY,
THE LANCASHIRE AND CHESHIRE COAL ASSOCIATION.

April, 1924.

The Colliery Guardian Co. Ltd., 30-31, Furnival Street, Holborn, E.C.4.

POSTER DETAILING THE 1924 PAY OFFER (Mr. & Mrs. Sumner)

12th. November 1856.
Henry Blundell and Robert Woods were killed, falling down the pit that they were walling.

From *'THE REPORT OF THE MINES INSPECTOR'*.
31st. January 1878.
While improperly passing over the small drum of a haulage engine when in motion Thomas Dwyer aged 65 years, a labourer, caught his foot, slipped and was crushed between the drum and the side wall.

SURFACE WORKERS AT ST. HELENS COLLIERY (St.HLH&AL)

POST OFFICE TELEGRAPHS.

No. of Telegram 1253

C or B

Recd. from CPD CRUTCH

9-13

By

Prefix   Handed in at   M.   Office of Origin and Service Instructions   Words   Received here at

LONDON Z   4C

J T BARRETT 18 XXGWX ARCHIBALD RD TUFNELL PARK N

TRADE UNION CONGRESS DECIDE TO SUPPORT MINERS EXECUTIVE
COUNCIL DIRECT ALL TRAM AND BUS MEMBERS NOT TO COMMENCE

WORK TUESDAY MORNING NEXT MAKE ARRANGEMENTS ACCORDINGLY

LETTER FOLLOWS ALL INSTRUCTIONS WILL BE ISSUED OVER MY
NAME

BEVIN TRANSUNION

JACKDAW NO. 105 GENERAL STRIKE   PRINTED IN GREAT BRITAIN

TELEGRAM FROM BEVIN CALLING THE STRIKE

record the events in the town of that terrible and yet exciting time.

16th. April 1926.
MINING CRISIS.
May be disaster in a fortnight.
Miners meeting at Sutton.

20th. April 1926.
PIT HEAD NOTICES.
Offer of best terms possible.

The T.U.C called the General Strike for 4th. May 1926. *THE ST.HELENS REPORTER* for that date:-
THE CRISIS.
How St.Helens will carry on.
Lighting, Power and Coal rationed.
Volunteers being enrolled.

The 'REPORTER' appeared on the 26th. May as a small single sheet of paper headed 'THE ST.HELENS

REPORTER. NATIONAL CRISIS NEWS BULLETIN NO 1'.

By 14th. May the General Strike had been called off. The 'REPORTER' was back to it's normal size. The miners stayed out on strike and a long bitter struggle began that left it's mark on the town.

From *'THE ST.HELENS REPORTER'.*
14th. May 1926.
MINERS MEETING.
Picturedrome commandeered for meeting.

18th. May 1926.
STORY OF RED GATE BRIDGE.
Midnight traffic hold up.
Serious charge against local miners.

21st. May 1926.
HAYDOCK AND THE CRISIS.
Feeding the children.

23rd. May 1926.
THE DISTRESS.
Guardians emergency plans.
Startling Relief figure,.
Unemployment nearly doubled.

Pamphlets appeared all over the country in appeals to help the families of miners.

Local colliers found it hard to feed their families and to keep them warm but the Lancashire collier was a very resourceful man.

THE
BRITISH WORKER
OFFICIAL STRIKE NEWS BULLETIN

Published by The General Council of the Trades Union Congress

No. 1.   WEDNESDAY EVENING, MAY 5, 1926.   PRICE ONE PENNY

WONDERFUL RESPONSE TO THE CALL

General Council's Message : Stand Firm and Keep Order

The workers' response has exceeded all expectations. The first day of the great General Strike is over. They have manifested their determination and unity to the whole world. They have resolved that the attempt of the mineowners to starve three million men, women and children into submission shall not succeed.

All the essential industries and all the transport services have been brought to a standstill. The only exception is that the distribution of milk and food has been permitted to continue. The Trades Union General Council is not making war on the people. It is anxious that the ordinary members of the public shall not be penalised for the unpatriotic conduct of the mineowners and the Government.

Never have the workers responded with greater enthusiasm to the call of their leaders. The only difficulty that the General Council is experiencing, in fact, is in persuading those workers in the second line of defence to continue at work until the withdrawal of their labour may be needed.

WORKERS' QUIET DIGNITY

The conduct of the trade unionists, too, constitutes a credit to the whole movement. Despite the presence of armed police and the military, the workers have preserved a quiet orderliness and dignity, which the General Council urges them to maintain, even in the face of the temptation and provocation which the Government is placing in their path.

To the unemployed, also, the General Council would address an earnest appeal. In the present fight there are two sides only—the workers on the one hand and those who are against them on the other.

Every unemployed man or woman who " blacklegs " on any job offered by employers or the authorities is merely helping to bring down the standard of living for the workers as a whole, and to create a resultant situation in which the number of unemployed must be greater than ever.

The General Council is confident that the unemployed will realise how closely their interests are involved in a successful issue to the greatest battle ever fought by the workers of the country in the defence of the right to live by work.

MESSAGE TO ALL WORKERS.

The General Council of the Trades Union Congress wishes to emphasise the fact that this is an industrial dispute. It expects every member taking part to be exemplary in his conduct and not to give any opportunity for police interference. The outbreak of any disturbances would be very damaging to the prospects of a successful termination to the dispute.

The Council asks pickets especially to avoid obstruction and to confine themselves strictly to their legitimate duties.

EXCERPT FROM T.U.C. BRITISH WORKER No. 1

Womens Committee for the Relief of Miners Wives and Children.

They need your help!

In the coalfields, hundreds of children are born every week into houses where dire poverty reigns. The mothers are weakened by anxiety and under-nourishment. They are often without baby clothes, and they have no money to buy them ; they lack proper clothing and bedding for themselves. We are trying with your help to send them food and clothing, soap and other necessaries.

In many a home there is not a penny to pay for light, so that the sick children cannot be properly tended at night.

The little children are running on the rough roads with broken boots or barefooted, their soft feet cut by the stones.

There is not enough money to get the young ones fresh milk, and the sudden heat wave will bring the dreaded summer sickness, the scourge of ill-fed little ones, in its train.

Will you help us to provide for these small children and their mothers ?

WOMEN'S COMMITTEE FOR RELIEF

PLEASE PASS ON THIS COPY OR DISPLAY IT

The British Gazette

Published by His Majesty's Stationery Office.

No. 8   LONDON, THURSDAY, MAY 13, 1926.   ONE PENNY.

GENERAL STRIKE OFF

UNCONDITIONAL WITHDRAWAL OF NOTICES BY T.U.C.

Men To Return Forthwith.

SURRENDER RECEIVED BY PREMIER IN DOWNING STREET.

Negotiations To Be Resumed In The Coal Dispute.

NO RESUMPTION BY MINERS.

Mr. Cook And End Of The General Strike.

"Nothing To Do With Us."

Following upon a meeting of the Miners' Federation Committee yesterday morning the following telegram was sent to all the coal-fields :—

"Miners must not resume work pending the decision of the National Conference convened for Friday next at the Kingsway Hall, London, 10 a.m. Please send delegates.—Cook, Secretary."

The Miners' Executive sat in conference for the greater part of the afternoon and eventually adjourned until ten o'clock this morning. After the adjournment Mr. A. J. Cook made the following official statement, explaining that it was the Miners' reply to the proposals put before them by the T.U.C. on Tuesday night :—

" In view of the statement made in the T.U.C. draft received after they had met Sir Herbert Samuel, the miners discussed the same and passed the following resolution :—

" 'That the Miners' Executive have given grave and patient consideration to the draft proposals prepared by the T.U.C. Negotiating Committee and endorsed by the General Council representing what they call the best terms which can be obtained to settle the present crisis in the coal industry. The Miners' Executive regret the fact that no opportunity for consideration was afforded the accredited representatives of the Miners' Federation on the Negotiating Committee in the preparation of the draft or in the discussions of May 11 leading thereto.

" ' At the best the proposals imply a reduction of the wage rates for a large number of mine workers, which is contrary to the repeated declarations of the Miners' Federation and which they believe their fellow trade unionists are assisting to resist. They regret, therefore, whilst having regard to the grave issues involved that they must reject the proposals. Moreover, if such proposals are submitted as a means of calling off the general strike, such step must be taken on the sole responsibility of the General Council of the T.U.C.'

MINERS NOT CONSULTED.

" At a meeting of the Executive of the Miners' Federation, held at Russell Square this morning, the following Resolution was passed :—

" ' That after hearing the report of the representatives of the T.U.C., we re-affirm our resolution of May 11 and express our profound admiration of the wonderful demonstration of loyalty as displayed by all workers, who promptly withdrew their labour in support of the miners' standard, and undertake to report to the conference to be convened as early as practicable.' "

Mr. Cook added : " In regard to the T.U.C. decision to call off the General Strike, that was decided without consultation with the Miners' Federation, and we were not parties to it in any shape or form. As far as the future is concerned, we shall give a full report of all that has taken place to our conference, and the delegates themselves will decide what action they will take.

" They will either make a decision at that conference or refer the matter back to the rank and file in the coal-fields. Until that is done I do not intend to make any further statement in regard to the position, believing that it is my duty to report first fully all that has happened to the miners who will be affected by the future negotiations.

" The decision of the T.U.C. has nothing to do with us. It was not in consultation with us. Our men will have to decide what they will do in the light of the T.U.C. decision. Our stoppage may continue for an indefinite period."

The coal owners are taking immediate steps to reopen negotiations.

POSTAL SERVICES.

Delivery Of Parcels To Be Resumed.

The Postmaster-General announces that the inland and foreign parcels post, which has been suspended during the strike, is being resumed this morning, and that the limitation of the weight of packets sent by letter or printed paper post to eight ounces is now removed.

Normal arrangements for the delivery and despatch of mails will be resumed as the usual railway and other transport services are restored.

EXCERPT FROM THE BRITISH GAZETTE 13TH MAY 1926

1st. June 1926.
PETTY PILFERING.
Thefts of wood and coke.

There were mass meetings of local miners.

25th. June 1926.
ST.HELENS MINERS MASS MEETING.

After this meeting a reporter quoted a collier as saying, "Would to God that Strike wus o'er'

9th. July 1926.
MEMORABLE THRONG AT PEASLEY CROSS.
Mr. H.A.Cook's visit to St.Helens.
Mass meeting of local mine workers.

Mr Cook was the General Secretary of the Miners Federation of Great Britain.

From *'THE ST.HELENS REPORTER'*.
13th. July 1926.
ONE IN FIFTEEN THOUSAND.
A tour of the St.Helens coalfield yesterday showed everything to be quiet everywhere. The only thing calculated to make any excitement was at the Parr pits of Messrs. Evans and Company which had the

'WORKING ON A DROP' (St. Helens Reporter)

Bad Organisation.

Organisation and Profits of the Coal Industry.

The Report of the Samuel Commission admits the bad organisation of the industry.

It admits that the Colliery Companies transfer coal at low prices to concerns in which the Collieries or their directors have substantial financial interests.

It admits that the distribution of coal is badly organised, and that there is too wide a margin between price at the pithead and price to the consumer.

It admits that the royalty owners take six and a-quarter million pounds a year from the industry—equal to 2s. a week from the wages of every man and boy employed.

It admits that in addition to all this the mineowners took a total of £232,000,000 in profits between 1914 and 1925.

Cut out the Parasites!
Nationalise the Industry!

P.T.O.

MINERS' LEAFLET

distinction of getting the signature of the only man in St.Helens out of 15,000 colliery workers to sign on for the first day of reopening.

There were many leaflets printed and circulated as the warring factions tried to put over their case to the general public.

27th. July 1926.
LONG SERIES OF THEFTS.
Coal and Timber are the lodestone.
Many Fines.

THE GREAT "HOLD-UP"

T.U.C. Threat to the Nation

STORY OF THE STRIKE.

What is the General Strike about?

The story is soon told.

I.   Eight months ago the Government appointed a Royal Commission to report on the coal industry. It also gave a subsidy to keep the industry going while its Commission sat.

II.   The Commission reported that "a disaster is impending over the industry", as 7 out of every 10 tons of coal are being produced at a loss. It also saw a revision of wages was needed to save the industry.

III.   The Government accepted the Report. The Coal Owners have accepted it. The miners refused to work a second longer or take a penny less even as a **temporary** measure to prevent ruin.

IV.   The Government strove day and night to secure an agreement. While negotiations were going on, the Trade Union Council (without consulting the workers) issued notices for a General Strike which would paralyse transport, factories, public services, printing works, and the entire business of the Country.

V.   Under this intolerable threat of a national "hold-up", the Government stood firm. It told the T.U.C. that they would not renew negotiations until the General Strike was called off.

VI.   The Government then put in force its plans for maintaining food and milk supplies. It called upon all loyal people to offer help, to stand together in meeting the "surrender or starve" challenge.

VII.   As Mr. Baldwin said, "the Government found itself challenged with an alternative Government." This alternative Government is a small group of trade union leaders. It represents only a small section of the people. It did not even consult that section before it held its pistol at the head of the Government.

THE GOVERNMENT STANDS FOR THE PEOPLE—THE PEOPLE WILL STAND BY THE GOVERNMENT.

THE GREAT 'HOLD UP'

CHALLENGE the CAPITALIST OFFENSIVE

Support the Miners

THE UNITED CAPITALIST FRONT

Mr. Stanley Baldwin in July, 1925 stated on behalf of the Government that "the wages of all workers must come down."

The Mine-owners' proposal to reduce wages and lengthen hours with the assistance of the government was only delayed by the solidarity of the Trade Union Movement last July.

The Coal Commission in its report states that wages must be reduced.

THE MINERS' CASE

The Miners so far have only asked that no reduction of wages nor lengthening of hours should be imposed upon them. This is borne out by their slogan "Not a penny off the pay ; Not a minute on the day."

REMEMBER BLACK FRIDAY 1921

When the miners were deserted by the rest of the workers and their leaders, and left to battle alone, their ensuing defeat was the prelude to the defeat of all sections of the working class : engineers, transport workers, railwaymen, etc.

REMEMBER RED FRIDAY 1925

The United Front of all workers on July 31st, 1925 in defence of the miners compelled the mine-owners and the Government to retreat temporarily to re-form their new forces behind the Coal Commission.

RENEWAL OF THE OFFENSIVE

Since Red Friday the Government and the capitalist class, with the creation of the O.M.S. and Special Constabulary, have been preparing to renew the offensive. The Coal Commission was the means to hide the active preparations for the attack. The capitalist objective is the same as in 1921—*reduction of wages* and imposing further burdens on the workers.

THE COMMUNIST PARTY AND THE UNITED FRONT

In 1921 the miners were defeated by the lack of unity and in 1926 the capitalist class seek to destroy that unity and solidarity of Red Friday by dividing the ranks of the working class.

No Party in this country has kept the lessons of Black Friday (1921) more clearly and consistently before the workers than the Communist Party—the Party which led the way to the "Back to the Unions" campaign, for "More Power to the General Council," for the "Industrial Alliance" to unite miners, railwaymen, transport workers, engineers, etc. in preparation for the capitalist offensive.

The Communist Party again appeals for complete solidarity of the working class in support of the miners. Insist that the General Council assumes command of a united trade union movement in support of the miners. Set up all-inclusive local Councils of Action under the auspices of the Trades Councils.

All together in defence of the Miners !

Smash the Capitalist Offensive !
Miners Must Have Guaranteed Minimum Cost of Living Wage !
Nationalise Mines with Workers Control !

Published by the Communist Party of Gt. Britain, 16 King St., Covent Garden London, W.C.1.
Printed by The Dorrit Press, Ltd. (T.U. throughout), 68 & 70, Lant St., Borough, London, S.E.1.

CHALLENGE OF THE CAPITALIST OFFENCE

Sleepers stolen at the dead of night.

30th. July 1926.
MINERS STEAL TELEGRAPH POLE
Curious theft at Sutton.
The Strike has hit us hard.
Colliers raid woods at Bold with hatchets and saws.

Coal picking on the colliery tips went on and it was not without it's dangers.

6th. August 1926.
CLOCKFACE COLLIERY MORNING SCENES.
Three men in a near escape.
The management of the colliery and the

Police gave permission for them to pick coal from the tip. The work was in full steam when the Manager said that they had started before the time. The Police were there and part of the tip fell burying three men, one of whom was covered up to the neck but removed alive. By eight o'clock the crowd had disappeared.

The Strike was becoming more bitter.

10th. August 1926.
CLOUDED LOOMING IN THE ST.HELENS COALFIELD.
Tinkler M.P. utters strong warning.
Threat to withdraw safety men.

OFFICE WORKERS AT A COLLIERY DURING THE STRIKE (Mr. Simm)

HAYDOCK MINERS 1926 (Mrs Bentham)

10th. August 1926.
RAID OF COAL AT ASHTONS GREEN.
16 Pilferers charged.
Safety Coal taken.

Despite the hardships that people endured all was not gloom. The photograph is of three Haydock colliers during the strike. They are, seated from left to right, Jack Hazelden, Harry Hatton and Albert Mesham. The man on the far left is believed to be Jack Bradshaw.

13th. August 1926.
PARR MINERS IMPROMPTU CARNIVAL.
Cheerful philosophy over the strike.

It is on record that the management of the collieries had the office staff working down mines. The photograph on the previous page is believed to be office workers at a Haydock colliery but which one the authors do not know. Notice the police officer in the background.

24th August 1926.
EXCITING MORNING AT SUTTON MANOR.
Interview with the manager.
What is peaceful picketing?

The more resourceful colliers opened their own 'opencast mines' but they were never very far away from the everyday dangers of coal mining.

From **'THE ST.HELENS REPORTER'.**
27th. August 1926.
OUTCROP WORKERS BURIED.
Fatality at Haydock.

The painful cessation was occasioned on Friday afternoon at Haydock when, in a fall of earth, four miners engaged in getting outcrop coal, were buried. Two were dead when extricated. They were William Cunliffe and Thomas Abbott of West End Road. Those got out were Thomas Harrison of 21, West End Road and John Melia of Regent Avenue Haydock.

The inquest was held at the Waggon and Horses at Haydock by Mr. S. Brighouse, the County Coroner. Jas. Cunliffe West End Road, collier and father of William, gave the evidence of identification. He said when he got to know of the accident he rushed to the spot just in time to see the fall and both bodies recovered. He said William left home at 11.15 am. and that was the last time he saw him alive.

Thomas Harrison, one of the injured men, gave evidence said he got out the spot along with the rest at 12.15 am and went under with Melia. The fall buried the two men and the mouth of the opening. There was another fall shortly afterwards. They were extricated and he and Melia were taken to the Cottage Hospital.

William Heyes, collier of West End Road stated he heard a crack and shouted 'Eigh up' but they had no time to get out of the way. P.C. Dibbs, who was on duty at Haydock that day, said he went along with six officers to prevent 'outcropping'. He heard shouting and then he saw men with spades from the Old Garswood Farm and after the two bodies had been extricated, they recovered Harrison and Melia. They had been buried about two hours. The two were treated for shock and minor injuries and have now been discharged.

The Coroner said he had received a message that the two were dead and he had made great speed to get the bodies released for burial. He was very sorry that these two had come to their deaths under these circumstances and everyone in Haydock would join him in expressing his sorrow. 'I am not looking for a matter of legal

RUBBING STONE COLLIERY (Mr. Simm)

standpoint. We must look at these matters from the standpoint of human nature. These fellows are out on strike, so they naturally go to the outcrops and get some coal. It may be against the Law but I do not express any opinion about it. If I had been in their places I would probably have done what they did.' The formal verdict was 'Misadventure'.

The strike was getting more violent.

14th. September 1926
PUGILISTIC THREATS AT SUTTON.
Blacklegs turn the tables.
Remarkable statement at Miners Meeting.

5th. October 1926
ST. HELENS POLICEMAN MAULED.
Furious scuffle in a passage.
Incidents of a coal case.

A Haydock collier, Mr. Felix McElroy who now lives in America remembers, 'The biggest demonstration was at Southport pit when hundreds of police charged the pickets on horseback and on foot. There were battles along the canal and some got pushed into the water. They chased us up Station Road with the horses and there were fights there'.

SUTTON HEATH & LEA GREEN COLLIERIES LIMITED.

11th SEPTEMBER, 1926.

The Company have posted notices at the Pits of the terms upon which all workpeople who were employed by the Company immediately prior to the stoppage will be signed on for work as it becomes available. These terms are :—

(1) One hour per shift more for surface and underground workers manipulating coal than before the stoppage.

(2) The same wages as before the stoppage will be paid, i.e., 66.66% on 1911 basis until 31st March, 1927.

Subsistence allowances awarded under the 1924 Agreement until the same date.

The 13.1% paid to piece workers will be discontinued.

(3) From April 1927 wages will be governed by the ascertained results of working in the months of December 1926 and January and February 1927, but the minimum percentage below which wages cannot fall will be 32% on the 1911 basis rates, and the subsistence allowances awarded under the 1921 agreement will be paid.

Further details will be found on the notices which have been posted at the Pits.

(Signed) JAS. ROBINSON,
Agent.

SAME WAGES
ON 8 HOURS
UNTIL 31st MARCH, 1927.

POSTER DATED 11TH SEPTEMBER 1926 (Mrs. Sumner)

12th. October 1926.
ROUND THE COALFIELDS YESTERDAY.
Back to work in the St.Helens pits.
The flowing tide begins.

Notices were posted at the pit heads of the terms that the companies would take on workers.

The strike was over and the colliers went back to work. Mr. McElroy again, 'When the strike was over (we lost). Everyone came out to cheer us as we walked to work'.

A few years later, the disillusionment of the experience and the economic state of the coal industry drove Mr.McElroy and many others to a new life in a new world.

Some of the effects of the Strike on the coal owners can be seen from the Minutes of the Meeting of the Directors of the Sutton Manor Colliery.

SUTTON HEATH & LEA GREEN COLLIERIES LIMITED.

The Pits in connection with these Collieries, SUTTON HEATH, LEA GREEN, KING, QUEEN and SHERDLEY will be OPEN FOR WORK on and from Friday next, 15th October.

All Men will be paid a

BONUS of 10/- for work done on Friday
do. 5/- do. Saturday
do. 5/- do. Monday

Women and Boys will be paid a "Bonus" of half these rates.

THE ABOVE BONUSES WILL BE PAID EACH DAY ON COMPLETION OF THE DAY'S WORK.

In addition thereto each Householder will receive, as a free gift, 1 cwt. of Coal.

All Wages will be made up to Monday night, 18th October, and will be paid (as usual) on Friday, 22nd October.

Signed,

JAMES ROBINSON,
Agent.

13th October, 1926.

POSTER DATED 13TH OCTOBER 1926 (Mrs. Lever)

Minutes of Meeting No. 181 of the Directors of The Sutton Manor Collieries Limited held at the Hotel Victoria, London on Wednesday, October 27th 1926, at 3.0 o'clock, p.m.

Attendance:

Present :-

Colonel Pilkington, in the chair, together with Mr. Preston, Sir Wemyss Grant-Wilson, Mr Gaskell, Mr. Gardiner and Mr. Lomax. Colonel Spencely was not able to be present, and Mr. Barker was prevented from attending through a cold. The Secretary was also present.

Mr. Cheetham's Written Report.

Mr. Cheetham's written report was read, stating that the number of men employed at October 25th above and below ground was 245.

The men returning to work had grown to a number which it is impossible to feed on the colliery premises, and it was therefore decided to let them go home daily, and to find means of conveying them. Accordingly, on October 5th a Daimler bus with seating accommodation for 26 had been purchased for £125. The bus had continued to run throughout the month, and about 75 people were conveyed from Farnworth and 30 from St. Helens each day. The running of the bus had a good effect on other men, as also had the selling of coal at the Colliery Yard. Later it was found necessary to finance a local Coal Dealer to the extent of £50 in the purchase of a Ford Van which was also being used as a conveyance of men to and from the Colliery. since then, the firemen and the enginemen have been able to go to their homes under police protection, but colliers and other underground workers have been billeted in.

During this time, the colliery was very closely picketed, and men who stood their ground had had a good deal to put up with, several of their homes having windows broken and walls white-washed.

Since the beginning of September, however, a small number of men had returned to work, and a total of 1,163 tons had been got and sent away.

The condition of the mine was fair considering the length of time they had been standing. Ventilation and water had been dealt with satisfactorily.

Mr Gardiner mentioned, also, that during the strike all the boilers and flues had been cleaned and inspected, and all the mechanical and electrical plant had been thoroughly overhauled and inspected.

Mr Cheetham said the office staff and all the members of the colliery staff had worked well, and given every assistance it was possible in the difficult days of the strike.

After hearing Mr. Cheetham's Report and the views of Colonel Pilkington, it was the unanimous desire of the Board to record their great appreciation of the splendid services remembered by Mr. Cheetham, his Officials and the Office Staff, and to congratulate them upon the satisfactory results achieved throughout the difficult and anxious days of the stoppage.

The position was improving gradually when unfortunately the meeting held by Cook in St. Helens had a noticeable effect in the Village, and stopped the inflow of men though it had not reduced the number of men working.

The coal faces though long standing were becoming affected, and in one seam the floor had lifted as much as 2 feet up the coal face, whilst in another the roof had broken off and sunk down one foot setting the coal in both cases.

Output of coal which has been quietly improving reached 996 tons for the week ending October 16th.

Mr. Cheetham also reported that at the beginning of October a bonus was offered to any person commencing work during the week for which the offer was made, and the number of men who accepted was such that the offer was extended for another week. He thought, however, it was desirable to continue the bonus, as if it got about that the bonus was not now to be paid it might have a deterring effect on the return of men to work.

It was resolved -

That the bonus so far paid be confirmed and that it be left with Mr. Cheetham to deal with bonuses in other cases as that arose.

Mover Colonel Pilkington, seconder Mr. Preston.

Police Protection.

Another thing which happened to interfere with the inflow of men was the rumour that the Liverpool Police were going to be removed, the effect was noticed in the Village, and Mr. Cheetham was quite sure that if they had been taken away the colliery would have had to close down.

In regard to this matter, the Secretary reported that when it came to his knowledge that police protection was to be withdrawn, although no official notice had been served on the Company, he got in communication with Sir Wemyss Grant-Wilson as quickly as possible and explained the position and the dangers which would arise.

Sir Wemyss had at once got in touch with the Home Office, who got in touch with the Watch Committee, as a result of which the decision to withdraw the Police was suspended pending an enquiry by the Home Office. it had been thought desirable that Mr. Cheetham, along with the managers of Bromilow Foster & Co. Limited and Richd Evans & Co. Limited, should send a report to the Chief Constable of the various events which have occurred since the outbreak of the strike, and the police protection required in cases of intimidation, and that Mr Cheetham should be ready to attend the enquiry on Friday next which was being held at the Town Hall St. Helens by Sir Leonard Dunning. It was felt that everything should be done to prevent any withdrawal of the police, and Sir Wemyss Grant-Wilson undertook to let the Home Office know that the reports of the Colliery Managers were being prepared and would be available as well as their personal evidence if desired.

FRANK KING & SID VINCENT, PRESIDENT OF LANCS. N.U.M. LEADING MARCH

MINERS, THEIR WIVES AND CHILDREN MARCH PAST THE TOWN HALL

CENTRE WILL ORGANISE FOOD SUPPLIES (Photos from St. Helens Reporter)

ARTHUR SCARGILL ADDRESSING MINERS AT BOLD

THE MINERS' STRIKE, 1984-85

1984-85 saw a bitter dispute with the coal industry nationally. It was a long dispute that wounded the town and left many scars, many of which are still in the process of healing.

SUTTON HEATH COLLIERY

The colliery was situated at the corner of Sutton Heath Road and Eltonhead Road. This colliery was mentioned in the 'Inspector's Report' for 1873, when it is shown as having two pits. At that time it was under the ownership of James Radley. The 1888 Report shows that it had passed to his widow Mrs. F.P. Radley. In the 1890's it was part of the Sutton Heath and Lea Green Collieries Co. Ltd., when the manpower was about 140. For many years, during this century, it was used as a pumping pit.

From *'THE REPORT OF THE MINES INSPECTOR'.*
26th. July 1867.
John Lea aged 26 years, a collier, was killed by an explosion of gunpowder.

From *'THE REPORT OF THE MINES INSPECTOR'.*
29th. November 1891.
At 5 pm. in the 11th. hour of the shift William Gee aged 19 years a drawer had stayed for some overtime with seven other men to clean the main haulage brow. He disturbed the foot of a prop supporting a large stone which fell between two slips and killed him.

OLD LADY, ELIZABETH GILL, SUPPORTING THE MINERS (St. Helens Reporter)

PICKETS ALLOWED THROUGH THE LINE OF POLICE TO SPEAK TO COLLEAGUES ARRIVING ON COACHES FOR THE AFTERNOON SHIFT AT PARKSIDE (St. Helens Reporter)

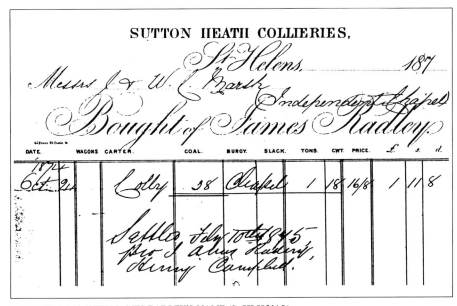

BILL HEADING WITH JAMES RADLEY'S NAME (St.HLH&AL)

From 'THE REPORT OF THE MINES INSPECTOR'.

1909.

In the No. 2 pit Hugh Jones aged 30 years and John Jones aged 45 years, both sinkers, were killed. The scaffold was supported by two ropes in the shaft which they were widening. They had three plugs let into the side of the shaft but the platform tilted and the two fell 60 yards to the bottom of the shaft and were killed. At the enquiry it was recommended that three capstan ropes should be fitted and not two.

The slogan was an the side of the coal tip at the colliery for many years and had to be removed during the Second World War as part of the Air Raid Precautions.

Pitmen took a pride in their skills and took time to pass examinations to get on in their work. The qualification also earned them more money.

A contractor in the mine would do the every day servicing of the mine in the 1920's. They would be paid by the colliery company and then they would pay the men that they employed.

An interesting little anecdote is brought to light, when on the back of the pay slips, it was the contractor's wife that worked out what was owed to the men.

WINDING HOUSE AND PIT HEADGEAR (St.HLH&AL)

CONTRACTOR'S WAGE PACKET & PAY SLIP

BURN LANCASHIRE COAL (Mr. Simm)

Sutton Heath & Lea Green Collieries, Limited.

Queen Pit.

Lea Green Mine.

No. **97**

3rd August 19**28**

COAL MINES ACT. 1911.

To *John Cunliffe*

You are hereby appointed as FIREMAN under the Act and General Regulations, of which a copy, in the prescribed form, is given to you with this Certificate, together with The S.H. & L.G.C. Co's. Instructions to Shotlighters.

Whilst making yourself acquainted with all these, your attention is particularly directed to the following :—

Coal Mines Act, 1911. Sections 14, 15, 34, 35, 37, 40 (4) (11), 44, 46, 47, 49, 50, 51, 52, 53, 55, 62, 63, 64, 65, 66, 67, 70, 71.

General Regulations 3, 8, 11, 12, 15, 16, 21, 22, 34, 49 to 62, 92, 96, 98, 99, 101, 104, 105, 110, 132, 133, 135.

Explosives in Coal Mines Order.

S. H. & L. G. C. Co's Instructions to Shotlighters.

On your leaving the occupation to which this Certificate applies you must return the Certificate.

Jos Robinson Manager

FIREMAN'S CERTIFICATE, 1928 (Mr. Sumner)

SUTTON MANOR COLLIERY

The colliery is situated on Jubits Lane. This is a modern colliery, that was only sunk this century, and is the only colliery still in production near to St. Helens town centre. The two shafts comprising Sutton Manor Colliery, were sunk between 1906 and 1912. A third shaft was started, but was subsequently filled in. In 1968, the colliery was reorganised, when coal production ceased in No.1 Pit and all work was concentrated in the more economic seams in No.2 Pit. The winding arrangements were changed in the 1980's, with new skip winding equipment being installed. The colliery is quite unique in having one of the newest winding engines in the country and also one of the oldest, still retaining the steam winder for men and materials.

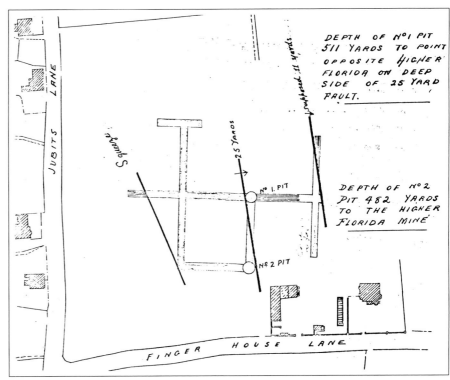

DEPTH OF Nº1 PIT 511 YARDS TO POINT OPPOSITE HIGHER FLORIDA ON DEEP SIDE OF 25 YARD FAULT.

DEPTH OF Nº2 PIT 482 YARDS TO THE HIGHER FLORIDA MINE

PLAN OF THE SINKING 1907 (Mr. Simm)

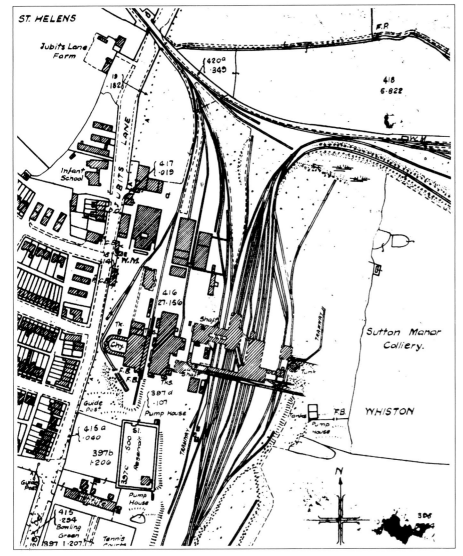

SURFACE PLAN OF SUTTON MANOR COLLIERY

From **'MR. JOHN ROBINSON'S REPORT TO THE DIRECTORS.'**
Liverpool 22nd. November 1907.

'Reported that No. 1 Pit, 18 feet dia., was now 400 yards down; that we should find the Potato Delf Mine at 480 yards and the Florida at 560 yards, reaching these in about 6 months time.

A sum of £35,000 will be required to be spent during the present year, made up as follows:-

Small Air Compressor	£210-0-0.
Balance on Generating set	£300-0-0.
Balance on Pit Headgear	£470-0-0.
Balance on Winding Engines	£2,175-0-0.
Winding Engine House	£500-0-0.
Pit Brow	£500-0-0.
Ropes	£300-0-0.
Rods	£400-0-0.
Catches	£150-0-0.
Boiler	£1,200-0-0.
Railway	£500-0-0.
Siding	£500-0-0.
Sinking and tunneling through 11 yard fault	£1,060-0-0.
Stores	£4,000-0-0.
Wages and Fees	£4,000-0-0.
Contingencies	£2,600-0-0.

Had these difficulties not been met with it is fair to assume that we should now have been raising a Get of 100 tons per day.'

EXCERPT FROM REPORT (Mr. Sumner)

SUTTON MANOR COLLIERY (SMM)

STEAM FAN ENGINE (SMM)

COMPRESSORS (SMM)

WINDERS CHAIR (SMM)

From *'THE REPORT OF THE MINES INSPECTOR'*.

20th. July 1908.

Frederick Tiplady aged 34 years, an erector, was engaged by a contractor to erect a new headgear when the chain they were using broke and he was fatally injured by a falling girder which they were trying to get into position.

The winders job is a solitary one, no-one being allowed in the winding house when he is working so he will have no distractions from his responsible job.

Compressed air has long been used to power underground machinery. It is supplied from large compressors, usually on the surface and fed down the shaft.

SUTTON
(PEASLEY CROSS)

The colliery was situated on the site of glassworks on Marshalls Cross Lane. The colliery appeared in the records of 1839 under the ownership of Bournes and Robinson, being one of the collieries that was connected to the St. Helens and Runcorn Gap Railway. It appears throughout the nineteenth century in the 'Inspector's Reports', becoming part of the Whitecross group of collieries in the latter part of the century. In the 1860's the production was given as 130,000 tons of coal per year. At the turn of the century manpower was about 250 men. The colliery closed in 1903.

UNION COLLIERY

There are references to two collieries of this name in the town.

UNION 1 was situated near Boundary Road and Knowsley Road. This colliery appeared in the 'Inspector's Reports' for 1850 and 1855, when it was in the ownership of James Radley. It does not appear any later than the early 1870's.

UNION COLLIERY 2. This was situated at the corner of Parr Street and Corporation Street. This colliery is recorded in 1823, when it was managed by Richard Johnson. It was reported as having closed in the 1840's, due to the coal recession of that year.

From *'THE REPORT OF THE MINES INSPECTOR'*
13th. May 1876.
John Topping, the banksman, aged 46 years was killed when he fell down the pit.

From *'THE REPORT OF THE MINES INSPECTOR'*
13th. February 1851.
T.Hayes was killed by a fall of roof in the No 7 pit. Two others injured.

VICTORIA COLLIERY

This was situated in Rainford and was first mentioned in the Inspector's Report in 1855. In 1879 it was owned by the Victoria Colliery Co. and was still working in 1888.

From *'THE WIGAN OBSERVER.'*
11th. December 1863.
There was a fatal accident at the Victoria Colliery, Rainford, when Peter Robinson was killed descending the shaft in the hoppet. The chain broke thirty yards from the top and he fell down the shaft.

From *'THE ST.HELENS STANDARD'.*
1st. January 1869.
Joseph Heaton, who worked at the Victoria Colliery at Rainford was charged under 'The Master and Servants Act' of leaving work without notice. He was fined 40/- with costs or if he could not pay, six months in jail.

WOOD COLLIERY

The colliery was situated on Vista Road, Haydock and was sunk in 1866 to a depth of 490 yards by Richard Evans & Co., and worked by this Company

AN EARLY VIEW OF WOOD COLLIERY

THE HAYDOCK COLLIERY EXPLOSION
1. Some Results of the Explosion. — 2. The Pit Brow : Volunteer Explorers Going Down. — 3. Bringing out the Body of One of the Victims. —
4. At Close Quarters : Testing the Ventilation. — 5. Mr. John Turton, Manager of the Pit, the First Rescuer.

until Nationalisation. This century its name was changed to Newton Colliery, but was later changed back. On Nationalisation, the colliery became part of the St. Helens Area and at that time produced about 200,000 tons of coal annually with a manpower of 875. The colliery closed in May 1971, when it was producing over 170,000 tons with a manpower of under 500.

From **'THE REPORT OF THE MINES INSPECTOR'.**
4th. April 1867.

John Whittle who was sinking a shaft at Wood pit was killed when a piece of rock fell from the sides which were well cased, rings having been placed to carry the walls every five yards down to the rock from which the missile came.

There was no proper foundation and the last eighteen yards which had not been cased. Rock often proves dangerous when not secured. If the four rings can not be laid in the usual way they should be lain on plugs of iron fastened to the sides of the pit.

THE WOOD PIT EXPLOSION.

The Wood Pit Explosion of 7th. June 1878 when some two hundred men and boys lost their lives, was the worst disaster in the Lancashire coalfield for many years and still stands as the most disastrous in the district.

Conditions underground were chaotic and it took several weeks to recover all the bodies. There was national interest in the explosion. Queen Victoria sent a telegram of sympathy to all those involved in the disaster and full page illustrations appeared in the Illustrated London News and The Graphic magazines.

John Turton, a Haydock man, was the manager of the colliery and showed great bravery in descending the pit on his own, immediately after the explosion and by his efforts saved between twenty and thirty men.

All the bodies were recovered though some were difficult to identify:-

Victim No.97 Peter Hughes, aged 37 years, a collier of Old Whint Road, Haydock who was identified from his pocket watch by Alice his wife who was left with four children. He was buried at St. James's, Haydock 16th. June 1878. Mr. Hughes' watch is still held by the family.

In Memory of
THE LATE
NATHAN BOON AND HIS FIVE SONS
Who lost their lives by the Wood Pit Explosion, Haydock.
JUNE 7th, 1878.

NATHAN BOON, AGED 45 YEARS
ISAAC BOON, AGED 21 YEARS,
JOHN BOON, AGED 20 YEARS.
THOMAS BOON, AGED 18 YEARS.
WILLIAM BOON, AGED 16 YEARS,
JOSEPH BOON, AGED 14 YEARS,

AND WERE INTERRED AT ST. THOMAS'S CHURCH, ASHTON.

REMEMBERANCE CARD FOR THE BOON FAMILY (Mr. Boon)

Remembrance card of funeral cards were produced for many of the victims and there are sill a few of these surviving today. The one for the Boon family is so sad, recording the fact that seven male members of the family were lost in the explosion.

A fund for the relief of the victims of the Haydock Colliery Disaster was set up under the chairmanship of Lord Derby, and collected about £25,000 by public subscription.

From **'THE REPORT OF THE MINES INSPECTOR'.**
10th. December 1888.

James Delaney aged 27 years, a drawer, was killed when another drawer was taking full tubs down the incline and the sprag broke. The tub overpowered him and ran into the deceased, who was going out with a loaded tub.

From **'THE ST.HELENS LANTERN'.**
25th. October 1891.

On Friday last John Canny aged 66 years was caught between the buffers of two waggons and crushed. He was taken to hospital and his leg was taken off. He is progressing favourably

From **'THE ST.HELENS LANTERN'.**
30th. March 1893.

Accidents in the Haydock collieries have been scarce of late but David Burnes a pony lad had the misfortune to break his arm on Monday and he is progressing favourably.

The collieries themselves were often a source of death and injury but the surrounding areas were a danger to the unwary.

IN MEMORY OF
THE UNFORTUNATE MINERS,
Killed by the Explosion at Wood Pit, June 7, 1878.

It is estimated that 204 have lost their lives by this awful Calamity, leaving 93 Widows and 282 Orphans.

Death did to them no warning give, | Take warning by their sudden fall.,
Therefore be careful how you live; | Let you for death prepare ;
Begin in time, make no delay, | For it will come ye know not when,
For no one knows their dying day. | The manner, how or where.

REMEMBERANCE CARD FOR THE EXPLOSION VICTIMS (St.HLH&AL)

HAYDOCK EXPLOSION RELIEF FUND.

CHAIRMAN OF THE GENERAL COMMITTEE

THE RIGHT HONOURABLE THE EARL OF DERBY, K.G.

VICE-CHAIRMAN

THE HIGH SHERIFF OF THE COUNTY OF LANCASTER, N. ECKERSLEY, Esq.

CHAIRMAN OF THE EXECUTIVE COMMITTEE.

LIEUTENANT-COLONEL GEORGE M'CORQUODALE.

SECRETARY

GEORGE L. CAMPBELL.

MAGISTRATES' ROOM,

NEWTON-LE-WILLOWS,

July 23, 1878.

The Worshipful the Mayor of St. Helens.

Joseph Cook Esq, &c, &c, &c.

Sir :

I have had the honour to submit your
letter of the 19th inst, addressed to Lord
Derby, to a meeting of my committee this
evening; and Mr. John Mercer, (Chairman
of the meeting,) and myself, have been
appointed a deputation to confer with
your worship as to its contents.

If convenient to you we can wait
upon you on Friday next at half past
Ten o'clock; if this appointment does
not fall in with your arrangements, will
you kindly fix some other time?

I have the honour to remain Sir,

Your very obedient servant.

Geo........

LETTER FROM RELIEF FUND (St.HLH&AL)

OLIVE RUCK, PIT BROW LASS (Mr. Hilton)

WOOD COLLIERY IN 1969

In 1898 the 'Workman's Compensation Act' became law and anyone injured at work could claim compensation from their employer. Compensation cases started to appear in the local press.

From **'THE NEWTON AND EARLESTOWN GUARDIAN'**
10th. February 1899.
COLLIERY COMPENSATION ACT.

In St. Helens County Court, Mr. H. L. Riley appeared before Judge Sands for leave to withdraw an action brought by James Jenkins, drawer of 70, Athol Street, Earlestown against Richard Evans and Company, with respect to an accident that happened to Jenkins while working in No. 1 Wood pit on the 27th. July.

The plaintiff claimed 15/- per week as compensation. Mr Riley said that it had been arranged between the plaintiff and the defendants that they should pay 10/- per week from the date of the accident to the present and to the end of the plaintiff's incapacity and also to pay costs. The Judge agreed and the case closed.

From **'THE NEWTON AND EARLESTOWN GUARDIAN'**.
19th. September 1898.
YOUTH DROWNED AT HAYDOCK.

Frederick Wardle aged 11 years, who lived with his parents in Lyme Street, was with some other boys on Sunday afternoon at the reservoir near Wood pit when the lad went into the water and disappeared. A lad

named Davis gave the alarm and a man came to the scene, dived in and brought up the boy's body.

At the inquest into the boy' death, John Hall, a labourer of Wood Pit Cottages Haydock, said that on that afternoon he was called to the colliery and recovered the body.

The jury brought in verdict of 'Accidentally drowned'.

A former Pit Brow Lass, Olive Ruck who worked at the pit in the late nineteen twenties relates, "My shift began at 7 am. and the first job was to wind the coal up to the surface of the mine itself. The coal and other sorts of horrid things was in large tubs which were 'womanhandled' down into a big yard where it was sorted by hand. And what mucky work it was. It was with relief that provision was made for twenty minutes breakfast, particularly as we worked in the open whatever the weather. Conditions weren't no better under cover either since the small wooden building where we ate our grub was festooned with rats. Small heads would pop up through cracks between the floor boards and noses would twitch at the hint of food.

After the break, it was back to work coal sorting, Hard dirty work all for 27/- a week. The work day finished at 3.30 pm. and then it was home to start the domestic chores".

Over the years the colliery was modernised but it never had it's own washery. The coal from the colliery was washed at Lyme Pit.

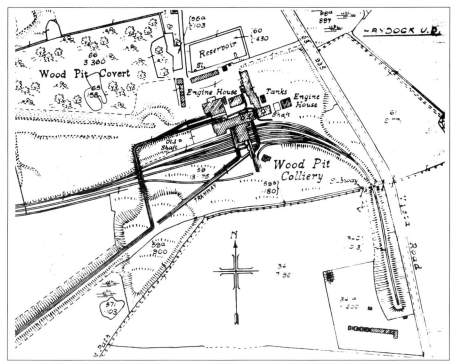

SURFACE PLAN OF WOOD COLLIERY IN 1952

THE GRANGE, HOME OF RICHARD EVANS (Mr. Simm)

DAVID BROMILOW

He was a large coal proprietor in the area who had interest in many collieries. One of his later companies was Bromilow Sothern and Co.

SARAH CLAYTON

She was a coal proprietor of Parr in the early eighteenth century and was involved in the great competition that went on over the Sankey Canal coal trade. It was through this that she went bankrupt in the 1770's. She will be remembered for the building of Clayton Square in Liverpool.

JOHNATHAN CASE

He was an eighteenth century coal proprietor who was related to Sarah Clayton. He was in competition with John Mackay and owned collieries in Sutton and Whiston.

CHARLES DAGNALL

He was a small coal proprietor in the 1740's and mined in Eccleston. He was generally known as a dishonest man.

BASIL THOMAS ECCLESTON

He was a local squire and landowner who was a miner himself in the eighteenth century but there is no record of him leasing land for coal mining.

RICHARD EVANS

He owned mines in Haydock and had interests in coal mines all over the district. He was head of the philanthropic family that built schools and churches all over the area.

DAVID GAMBLE

The famous industrial chemist was involved in many partnerships with coal owners in the district. A major contributor to the development of the town who was knighted in 1904.

THE GREENALL FAMILY

The famous local brewers who became St.Helens dignitaries were involved in coal mining at the Hardshaw Colliery.

RAVENHEAD HOUSE

JOHN MACKAY

He was a Scottish industrialist who played a great part in the industrial foundation of the town. His interests in coal were at Parr and Ravenhead and he lived at Ravenhead House which is still standing today. He also founded the Ravenhead Glass Works.

JOHN MIDDLEHURST

He was a local builder of churches and schools and mined coal on the Hardshaw Estate.

JAMES ORRELL

He was a coal master at the end of the eighteenth and beginning of the nineteenth centuries. His main collieries were situated in Blackbrook and Glade Hill. He lived in Blackbrook House that still stands today.

PILKINGTON BROTHERS

Richard and William Pilkington were the founders of the Glass Company and also coal proprietors. Later other members of the family took control of Richard Evans and Co. in the twentieth century.

JAMES RADLEY

He was a successful coal proprietor in St.Helens and later owned the Pocket Nook Smelting Co.. He was one of the first members of the St.Helens Corporation and was Mayor of the town in the 1870's. He died in 1885.

BLACKBROOK HOUSE (Mr. Simm)

GLOSSARY OF TERMS

Afterdamp
Poisonous carbon monoxide gas that is left in the mine after and explosion.

Banksman or Browman
The official of the colliery who is in charge of the pit head.

Brakesman
A man who rode on waggons on the surface and worked the brake.

Brattice
A wooden frame to which was nailed a heavy cloth to direct the ventilating air through the mine.

Bar
A horizontal piece of timber that supports the roof.

Brow
A tunnel usually used in the haulage of coal.

Capping
An old word for broken.

Cage
A kind of lift that transports men and materials up and down the shaft.

Chargehand
A foreman.

Chokedamp
A suffocating gas that if found in mines.

Coalpicking
Taking coal off the coal tips.

Contractor
A man who did the general servicing of the mine and employed other men.

Coupling chain
The chain that held the tubs together.

Crossover
A construction that took air currents or rails over each other.

Dataller
A day wage man.

Deputy
An official of the mine.

Dib hole
The hole at the bottom of the shaft. See Sump.

Drawer
A man or boy employed by the collier to take the coal away in boxes.

Dome shackles
The hooks on the top of the cage that enabled it to be taken out of the shaft.

Downbrow
With the slope of the coal

Downcast
The shaft down which the fresh air passed.

Endless rope
The haulage mechanism by which tubs were transported both above and below ground.

Engineman
The person in charge of an engine either at the surface or under ground.

Firedamp
Methane gas which can become an explosive mixture when mixed with air.

Fireman
An underground official of the colliery.

Furnace
The fire at the bottom of the upcast shaft that drew fresh air through the mine.

Furnaceman
A man who was in charge of the furnace, usually underground.

Gang
A train of coal tubs.

Goaf
The waste behind the coal from which the coal has been mined.

Gob
See Goaf

Headgear
The construction erected over the shaft.

Hooker-on or On-setter
The men in charge at the bottom of the shaft.

Hoppet
A large bucket that is raised and lowered in the shaft.

Horsekeeper
The man who looked after the pit ponies.

Jig
A pulley wheel in the haulage system, usually at the top of an incline.

Jigger
The person, usually a lad, who operated the jig.

Knock
A signal that was used to signal the cage in the early days of mining.

Manhole
See Refuge place.

Metalman
A man who got down rock and packed it in the waste or gob.

Mine
An old name for a coal seam.

Miners agent
The name given to an early union official.

Mines Inspector
A government official who inspected the mines. The first Inspectors reported in 1850.

Methane
See firedamp.

Mystagmus
A disease of the eyes that affects miners, when the eyes wander.

On-setter
See Hooker-on.

Ostler
A man who looked after the horses.

Overman
An old name for a deputy. See deputy.

Overwinding
The act of the cage being wound past it's normal stopping place at the surface.

Outcrop
Where a coal seam comes to the surface

Outcropping
The act of mining the coal near the surface.

Pit
Another name for the shaft.

Prop
A vertical piece of timber that supported the roof.

Pulled in

A local term for overwinding.

Refuge place

A hole cut in the side of a roadway so that men could get out of the way of tubs. (See manhole).

Rules

There are General and Special rules that apply to a colliery. Every man had to be given a copy when they were employed at the colliery and they were a job specification.

Screens

The mechanical riddles where the coal was graded at the surface.

Seam

A layer of coal. See mine.

Shaft

The vertical entrance to a mine. See pit.

Shotlighter

An official of the colliery whose job it was to fire the explosive charges.

Sinker

A man who dug shafts.

Sinking

The act of making a new pit.

Slip

A fault in the roof or coal.

Sprag

A short prop that was used to support the undercut coal.

Stoneman

See metalman.

Sump

See dib hole.

Sylvester

A ratchet chain with a lever used to remove props. (See gablock)

Tenter

Someone who looked after something.

Tramway

The rails in the haulage roads along which boxes were pulled.

Tub

A small wheeled vehicle that usually ran on rails and carried the coal underground.

Undermanager

An official in the pit.

Unramming

The act of taking out an unexploded charge.

Upcast

A shaft at the bottom of which, was the furnace.

Underlooker

An old name for a deputy on official in the mine.

Ventilation

The means by which fresh air is supplied to the mine.

Waggon

An old name for a tub.

Waggoner or Waggonman

An old name for a drawer.

Walling

The act of building walls from waste material.

Workings

The area of the mine where the coal was won.

Yicker

An inhabitant of Haydock.

INDEX OF MINING TERMS

INDEX OF SURNAMES